KING ALFRED'S COLLEGE
WINCHESTER

—

To be returned on or before the day marked
below :—

PLEASE ENTER ON ISSUE SLIP:

AUTHOR RODGON

TITLE Single-word usage

ACCESSION No. 63346

Single-word usage, cognitive
development, and the beginnings
of combinatorial speech

Single-word usage, cognitive development, and the beginnings of combinatorial speech

A study of ten English-speaking children

MARIS MONITZ RODGON

University of Illinois at Chicago Circle

CAMBRIDGE UNIVERSITY PRESS

CAMBRIDGE

LONDON · NEW YORK · MELBOURNE

Published by the Syndics of the Cambridge University Press
The Pitt Building, Trumpington Street, Cambridge CB2 IRP
Bentley House, 200 Euston Road, London NW1 2DB
32 East 57th Street, New York, NY 10022, USA
296 Beaconsfield Parade, Middle Park, Melbourne 3206, Australia

© Cambridge University Press 1976

First published 1976

Photoset in Malta by Interprint (Malta) Ltd

Printed in the United States of America by
Vail-Ballou Press, Inc., Binghamton, New York

Library of Congress Cataloguing in Publication Data

Rodgon, Maris Monitz.

Single-word usage, cognitive development, and the beginnings
of combinatorial speech.

Includes bibliographical references and index.
1. Children—Language.   2. Languages—Psychology.
I. Title.
P118.R6   401'.9   75-7211
ISBN 0 521 20884 X

TO JACK RODGON

Contents

Acknowledgements

The research and theory reported in this volume have been in the process of development for several years, and have been influenced by the thoughtful contributions of many persons. Much of the research reported here formed part of a doctoral dissertation conducted at the University of Chicago Department of Psychology under the direction of Professor David McNeill. I shall remain grateful for his suggestions and guidance over the years. I would also like to thank Professors Augusto Blasi, Barbara Lozar, and Joseph Wepman for their help at this stage. Also, thanks to Jon Jaffee and Carrie Levine for serving as observers.

The research reported here was conducted during the summer of 1971. Since 1972, I have been engaged in a longitudinal study of single-word speech at the University of Illinois at Chicago Circle. This study was partially supported by a grant from the UICC Graduate College Research Board. The results of the longitudinal study, and of several concurrent studies focusing on the relationship between language development and cognitive processes have influenced the theory presented in chapter 5 of this book. It would be impossible to acknowledge individually all the persons who have been associated with the project, but the following persons deserve special thanks: Wayne Jankowski, Lucias Alenskas, Sue Ellen Rashman, Lawrence Kurdek, and Marilyn Gans. I also extend my sincere appreciation to Kathleen Gallagher, Dawn Decker, and Ramona Robinson for their endless work on the manuscript. Finally, I would like to thank the people without whom this study could never have been done: Lia, Glynis, Deanna, Katie, Jordan, Jessica, Andrew, Ricky, Paula, and Felice, and their families. Working with all of them was an utter delight.

October 1974   Maris Rodgon

I Earlier work on the origins of language

Among the mushrooming number of studies of children's acquisition of language, increasing attention is being paid to the earlier stages of child speech (Bloom, 1970; Schlesinger, 1971; Brown, 1973). Most of this attention, has been focused on the earliest combinatorial speech. Recently, there have been several studies investigating the simplest beginnings of speech, the single-word utterances of the one- to two-year-old child (Smith, 1970; Greenfield, Smith, and Laufer, in press; Bloom, 1973; Nelson, 1973). This book is a report of both an investigation into the nature of single-word speech and its relationship to later combinatorial speech, and an investigation into the relationship between single-word speech and the child's cognitive development on the sensory-motor level, which should be occurring at about the same time. In order to place this research in proper perspective, it is necessary to first review previous studies of single-word speech and its possible connection to later language acquisition. Some of these studies have been performed or published since this investigation was begun. For this reason, they had no theoretical effect on its design and execution but the approaches, methods, and results, can still be compared. After this review, various theoretical positions regarding the connection between language acquisition and cognitive development will be presented, as they bear upon the hypotheses and experimental procedures involved in this study.

PREVIOUS STUDIES OF SINGLE-WORD SPEECH

Although there have been few studies of single-word speech by developmental psycholinguists until very recently, the phenomenon of single-word speech has been known and studied observationally for many years.

The following discussion will be organized around five issues, as they relate to the present study. First, a definition of the term 'holophrase' as it is used in this book, will be presented. Next, a short review of previous studies, oriented toward the definition of a 'holophrase' and the use of extralinguistic context in classifying utterances is included. This leads to the third topic, the validity of utilizing extralinguistic context in the classification of child speech. Fourth is a presentation of the types of linguistic relations which have previously been used in classifying child speech, as these relate to the classification system proposed in this study. Finally, there is a short discussion of the theoretical and empirical problems involved in an experimental investigation of single-word speech.

Definition of a 'holophrase' as used in this study

As employed here, the term 'holophrase' refers to a single-word utterance which is used by a child to express more than the meaning usually attributed to that single word by adults. As will be seen below, some previous investigators have used this term to refer to a single-word 'sentence', implying that the child through the use of only one word somehow conveys the semantic content which later will be contained in an entire grammatical sentence. As the term is used here, however, one need not assume that the child intends to communicate the meaning of an entire adult sentence, or that he understands the grammatical and semantic complexities of an entire sentence. Instead, a holophrase conveys the meaning of a consistent linguistic relation, as a linguistic relation will be defined below. This linguistic relation might or might not comprise an entire sentence. For example, the single-word utterance 'throw' might be analyzed through the use of extralinguistic context as the holophrastic expression of a subject–verb–object relation, 'Mommy *throw* the ball',[1] in which case the gloss is an entire sentence. In another case, the word 'Daddy' might be analyzed as the holophrastic expression of the possessive relation '*Daddy*'s shirt', in which case the gloss is only part of a sentence. The theoretical implications of this definition, as well as the methods by which utterances were actually classified will be discussed in detail in succeeding chapters.

Previous studies of single-word speech as they relate to the present study

The idea that the child who utters a single word is producing the functional equivalent of a larger linguistic unit, usually the sentence, has been discussed by many authors before the current impetus in developmental psycholinguistics (Stern and Stern, 1907; de Laguna, 1927; Leopold, 1949;

[1] This form of notation is borrowed from Smith (1970).

McCarthy, 1954; and others). More or less complete reviews of this work can be found in McNeill (1970b), Smith (1970), Greenfield et al. (in press), and Brown (1973). One point of special interest with respect to this study is that all the authors mentioned found evidence in the holophrastic period as they defined it for the existence of predication, various examples of the attribution of a property to an object or a situation. It is also of interest that none of these formulations was based upon experimental evidence. Support was provided by diary studies, notably one of a German-English bilingual (Leopold, 1949) and one of a French monolingual (Gregoire, 1949). A great deal of attention was given not only to demonstrating the predicative property of holophrastic speech, but also in illustrating the original connection with and later differentiation from the expressive function of speech (de Laguna, 1927; Leopold, 1949; Werner and Kaplan, 1963; McNeill, 1970b):

When one considers that the question of development during the single-word period is now highly controversial, the applicability of de Laguna's (1927) early observations is striking. She claims that during the approximately six-month period in which they are used, not only do single-word utterances undergo considerable development, but that this development can only be understood by adults in terms of the contexts in which the utterances are produced. The sequence begins with the child using a gesture to name an object. Then he replaces this gesture with a name-word. The introduction of words thus immediately increases his communicative capacity. After the name comes the sentential holophrase, a single word which communicates the idea of an entire sentence. In effect, the child is predicating something, i.e. commenting upon or remarking about the non-linguistic situation through the use of a single word. Soon this single word is accompanied by another gesture, and eventually that gesture is replaced by another word, so that the child is producing two-word utterances. This sequence could never have been recognized if either the types of situations which evoked utterances, or the accompanying gestures, had been ignored.

Werner and Kaplan (1963) discuss the development of predication in similar developmental terms. They use the term 'monoreme' instead of holophrase, and point out a progression in the use of monoremes from the earliest predications of reference or naming through predications of action and finally to predications of attribution. Werner and Kaplan stress the fact that development during the one-word stage, on both a syntactic and semantic level, is continuous with development of combinatorial speech.

Greenfield is another investigator who stresses the continuity of single-word and combinatorial speech. The first word spoken by Greenfield's daughter (Greenfield, 1968) which, incidentally, Greenfield deliberately taught her (Greenfield, 1967), was used in a general referential sense. Next the child became able to assert properties and then to use words apparently in grammatical relations. For example, when one considers the extra-linguistic context of the utterance, the single word which the child uttered might be viewed as the object of a preposition in a complete adult sentence. The use of extralinguistic context, and the various classification systems used in this and following studies will be discussed in detail in succeeding sections. Considering Greenfield's preliminary data, as well as other avail-able evidence, McNeill (1970b) concludes that the child intends from his earliest utterances to express a complete sentence, although at first this sentence meaning is inextricably fused with affect.

Since these early studies, there have been two analyses of holo-phrastic speech based upon data obtained by Greenfield. Smith (1970), in a preliminary analysis of much of the material later included by Greenfield, Smith, and Laufer (in press), was already able to trace systematic progressions in the use of holophrases. Smith's major con-cern was to account for the utterance of a single word in many dif-ferent situations, and the converse use of different uttered words to express the same underlying relation in similar situations. The types of syntactic and semantic relations which he studied will be discussed in the next section. Smith used the working assumption, later modified by Greenfield et al., that a holophrastic single-word utterance is the child's way of expressing some functional equivalent of an entire grammatical sentence. Using a system, which will also be described below, in which the extralinguistic context of an utterance was used to fit a sentential gloss to the single-word utterance, Smith was able to trace a progression in the types of glosses which can be applied. This progression begins with demands (Austin, 1965) or performatives, single words which accompany actions and cannot be expanded. One example is a child's word for 'thank you' which was uttered whenever the child gave or received an object. Next came holophrases which point to, indicate, or call attention to objects, such as 'record' or 'cookie', interpretable as 'This is a *record*', or 'There is a *cookie*'; the word in italic is the one actually expressed. After this came holophrases which at first glance appear to be naming behavior, but which really represent the sentence, 'I want *something*'. Last in the sequence are declarative sentences such as 'The *record* stopped.' Within this last group, Smith notes that first-person or 'ego-subject declaratives' such as 'I want to get *down*', appear first.

Since Smith was the first systematically to analyze speech during the holophrastic period, he was the first to document the assumption that changes in the system occur gradually. New words do not bring new structures, but fit into the structures already in use. Similarly, within the same structure, different words may be expressed. For example, Smith notes that 'fan' (I want the *fan* on) and 'on' (I want the fan *on*) 'differed only in which element of the sentence was expressed' (p. 55).

In the later analysis of much of this same data, Greenfield, Smith, and Laufer (in press), used a modified version of Fillmore's case relations in classifying the utterances, again as described below. With this more refined system, they were again able to document a longitudinal progression in the appearance and use of these various relations, both over the course of the holophrastic phase, and into the beginning of the combinatorial period. This apparent continuity between holophrastic and combinatorial speech is stressed as extremely important in understanding the total process of language acquisition.

Very recently, an extensive study of speech during the age range of ten to twenty-five months has appeared (Nelson, 1973). Nelson kept detailed records of vocabulary growth, marking what she felt to be milestones in the number of words and phrases used. She, too, utilized extralinguistic context in determining the meaning of an utterance. In classifying the types of words which children used during this period, Nelson focused on the communicative aspect of language, rather than grammatical or semantic structure. She does not deal with the issue of holophrastic relations as they might describe grammatical structures. Nelson was able to distinguish two groups of children according to their functional use of language. These groups were called referential, or object-oriented, and expressive, or interpersonally and communication-oriented. Nelson also included tests of language comprehension during this period. In addition to charting longitudinal changes in language usage, she was able to illustrate relationships between the various indicators she employed, and to propose their significance in terms of syntactic and semantic development.

There has been one study of single-word speech which purportedly shows that there is no phenomenon of holophrastic expression, or more specifically, that there is no evidence for the existence of linguistic relations during the single-word period (Bloom, 1973). Both Bloom (1970) and Brown (1973)[1] previously denied the existence of syntactic relations in the

---

[1] Brown (1973) includes an extensive discussion of the importance of the single-word period in terms of the child's awareness of *semantic* relations.

single-word period, based upon the obvious lack of evidence for fixed patterns of word order. In this study of a single child, her daughter Allison, Bloom's main contention is that changes in the child's cognitive modes of organizing his world and his experience are occurring simultaneously with the development of linguistic structure, and that before actual linguistic structure appears, words reflect these changes in cognitive organization. These ideas will be discussed below in the section considering the relation between language acquisition and cognitive development. Bloom makes other points, however, which are relevant here. She observes that many of Allison's single-word utterances seem to serve non-holophrastic purposes. For example, there is much simple naming. The fact that non-holophrastic usages exist, however, does not mean that there can be no holophrastic speech. None of the authors mentioned above or below claims that all single-word speech is holophrastic, but only that a large proportion of single-word speech can be usefully interpreted in this way. Bloom also mentions the existence of 'place-holders', or non-meaningful sounds which begin to appear in combination with single words. For example, Allison's use of 'widə', which apparently had no consistent meaning, may have been necessary to pave the way for combinatorial speech. Such an assumption implies that single-word speech is somehow not an adequate precursor to combinatorial ability.

One especially relevant point is the discussion of two-word 'sequences' of separated single words which precede true combinations for Allison, and for some other children. In previous investigations, Bloom proposed that the interchangeability of word order in these two-word sequences argued against their grammaticality. In considering Allison's speech, Bloom notes that the two words which appear in sequence usually have two different functions. She suggests that they are often interpretable according to the topic-comment formulation which will be described below; this would allow the variability in word order. Although this hypothesis is interesting, it does not exclude the possibility of holophrastic speech. As suggested below, the topic-comment formulation may prove useful in interpreting holophrases, as well as combinatorial speech.

There has been one other study involving the single-word speech of a single child. This is the Italian monolingual Claudia (Antinucci and Parisi, 1973). Like Greenfield, Antinucci and Parisi were interested in the continuity between single-word speech and combinatorial speech. They did find a progression which will be discussed in the section on the various types of relations which can be used to classify single-word speech.

The use of extralinguistic context in the classification of child speech

Actually, observers of children's earliest speech have been using extra-linguistic context in order to form judgements about what the child actually meant to say for many years. Most of the early investigators (Stern and Stern, 1907; de Laguna, 1927; Leopold, 1949; Gregoire, 1937; Werner and Kaplan, 1963) were at least implicitly aware of the importance of the child's intonation patterns, his gestures and facial expressions, and the events happening around him in the interpretation of the single words he uttered. Only de Laguna (1927) and Werner and Kaplan (1963), however, dealt explicitly with the relation between action and gesture and the words the child produced. Both of these stressed the importance of considering every-thing the child was doing at the time at which he was talking, and both were able to trace developmental progressions in the child's usage of single words. These progressions have been described above. In the light of these early findings, it is surprising that a controversy regarding the use of extra-linguistic context in classifying single-word utterances still exists today.

Of the recent investigators, Bloom (1970) has done most to legitimize the use of extralinguistic context in classifying very early combinatorial speech. By making use of events happening around the child at the time of an utterance, she was able to identify both syntactic and semantic regularities, as well as regular progressions in the use of these regularities with on-going development. As noted above, however, Bloom has reservations about the applicability of this method to the single-word period. Perhaps her biggest objection is that some of the strongest evidence for the existence of stable grammatical relations in combinatorial speech is based upon the invaria-bility of the word order in which these relations are expressed. Such evid-ence is by definition not available in cases in which only a single word is involved. Brown (1973) agrees with Bloom's (1970) conclusions that this method is not applicable to the single-word period.

As defined in this study, a holophrase has three parts: the single word uttered by the child, the non-linguistic context in which it was uttered, and the sentential expansion with which adults gloss the holophrase. The first two are hard data; they can be observed and recorded with reasonable objectivity. The gloss, however, the sentence or relation which can be re-garded as a paraphrase of the single word uttered, can never be conclusively proven to be an accurate representation of the meaning which the child intended to convey. The gloss, in fact, is some adult's theory of what the child meant by the utterance. Nelson (1973) cautions repeatedly that adults must not attribute their own mental structure to the child. It is crucial, then, to note that the joint consideration of single-word utterance and extralinguistic context reveals regularities over time in the types of sentential glosses which can be applied. These regular progressions, if replicable by different observers, should be considered to be legitimate data. Such progressions were found by Smith (1970) and by Greenfield, Smith, and Laufer (in press) and are one subject of the present study. The progressions which have been found have already been discussed; it is the method of utilizing extralinguistic context which remains to be briefly mentioned here.

Both Smith (1970) and later Greenfield, Smith, and Laufer (in press) attempted to note as much as possible of the total situational context of each utterance. Everything of which the child could have been aware was to be considered; judgements were made about which aspects of the situation were actually salient for the child. In Smith's case, since he believed that a holophrastic single-word utterance is the child's way of expressing some functional equivalent of an entire grammatical utterance, he utilized the extralinguistic context to determine which sentence the child might have intended. For example, one subject said 'eat', and after consideration of the context, including the immediately preceding events, this was interpreted as 'I want to *eat* something.' Greenfield et al. (in press) employed essentially the same system; the difference was that they classified the utterances as examples of a modified system of case relations rather than as entire sentences.

It is clear, then, that there are progressions in holophrastic usage which can be described if, and only if, the extralinguistic context is utilized in interpretation. Nelson (1973) also relies on context in interpretation although she does not use the term 'holophrase'. It is also true that the use of extralinguistic context in classifying combinatorial speech is now achieving fairly general acceptance (Bloom, 1970; Brown, 1973; McNeill, 1970b). This author accepts the evidence presented above that it is not only legitimate, but necessary to consider extralinguistic context; without it, one might completely miss the meaning of the child's single-word utterances. He would certainly, at least, be unaware of the changes in the types of single-word utterances over the course of this period in language acquisition.

Types of linguistic relations used to describe child speech and their applicability to the single-word period

Most recent investigators of child speech have been careful to distinguish between grammatical and semantic relations. For various reasons, they view language as relational with respect to grammar, and they also view two-word combinations as expressing only a limited number of semantic relations, i.e. a limited range of meanings. A variety of different types of 'relations' has been proposed. They are discussed here particularly in relation to their applicability to the description of relational single-word, and particularly holophrastic, speech.

The current impetus in the study of child language began in the early 1960s and was greatly influenced by Chomsky's (1957) generative transformational grammar. It was understandable, therefore, that the first investigators were looking for syntactic regularities in child speech. Three studies (Bellugi and Brown, 1964; Miller and Ervin, 1964; Braine, 1963) seemed to show regularities in the patterning of words in two-word utterances. At first the distributions were interpreted through the postulation of two word classes called 'pivot' words and 'x-word' or 'open' words (Braine, 1963). Apparently, there were two small non-overlapping classes of pivot words which occurred in fixed position, either first or second in a two-word utterance; a given child might display one or both of these pivot classes (Braine, 1963; Miller and Ervin, 1964). In addition there was also a large open class with many members. These open words were largely adjectives and nouns; they received their name because they could appear in the position left open by the pivot words. They could also appear alone, or in combination with each other.

It was originally proposed that these were generic classes which later became differentiated into the syntactic classes of the transformational grammar of English (McNeill, 1966). It has since been shown that such differentiation could not occur (McNeill, 1970a, 1970b; Bloom, 1970; Brown, 1973). McNeill (1970b) and Brown and his co-workers, instead see the analagen of adult syntactic relations in the early stages, and outline a progressive development of syntactic functions (McNeill, 1970b; Brown, Bellugi, and Cazden, 1968; Brown, 1973). It is primarily these syntactic relations, such as subject-predicate of a sentence, and modifier-head noun of a noun phrase, of which Bloom (1970) and Brown (1973) were speaking, when they claimed that word order provides good evidence for early grammatical relations.

Although Bloom's grammars (1970) were formulated largely in syntactic terms, she emphasized the necessity of including many semantic differentiations among the rules of the grammars. For example, nouns appearing in the Kathryn I and Gia I grammars were marked ± animate, a semantic distinction. Her grammars make use of semantic differences and contextual information to accommodate the possibility that two utterances with the same surface form have different grammatical representations, and in turn, serve different functions for the child. For example, Kathryn at stage I said 'Mommy sock' once to indicate possession, and once when Mommy was putting Kathryn's sock on Kathryn. The importance of this distinction is acknowledged in this study, and extended to the earlier stage of single-word utterances.

Although Bloom was a pioneer in the systematic semantic interpretation of children's utterances, many other schemes have recently been devised. Schlesinger (1971), for example, describes child linguistic performance in terms of a set of 'realization rules' with which the child implements his 'intention', diagrammed by an 'I-marker'. In other words, the child begins with something he wants, an intention, and utilizes a set of rules to transform this intention into a linguistic performance. The rules indicate the relative position of sentence components, as well as their grammatical classifications, but they are largely concerned with differences in meaning rather than grammar, and they do not describe the syntax in transformational terms (see Brown, 1973).

In his analysis of the development of single-word speech in three children, Smith (1970) was concerned with both syntactic and semantic relations, in a manner somewhat similar to that of Bloom (1970). For instance, he discusses both the semantic connection between actor–action–object and the syntactic connection between noun–verb–noun. As mentioned above, Smith's working assumption, that a holophrastic single-word utterance is the child's way of expressing some functional equivalent of an entire sentence, was later modified by Greenfield et al. (in press). One problem with Smith's original formulation was the empirical difficulty in determining which of a series of potential whole-sentence glosses really represented the meaning which the child intended. For example, the utterance 'light' as the child's mother turned the light out might be glossed 'Mommy turned the *light* out', or 'Mommy is turning the *light* out', etc. Smith claimed that the difference in the whole sentence was not important. In any case, the relation between the three words, 'Mommy', 'light', and 'out' remained the same. The Greenfield et al. formulation accepts this explanation and carries it one step further by assuming that the child intends to express the relation between these words, and not any one of the whole sentences. Nelson (1973) makes a similar claim, that single words, understood in context, convey a meaning different from the adult single-word meaning, but not that of an adult sentence.

Brown (1973) points out the possibility of using Fillmore's (1968) case grammar to describe child language. In this grammar a sentence is described as a proposition plus a 'modality description'. Limitations on form are expressed largely in terms of the cases of the nouns which can appear in the sentence. These cases are very similar to the usual description of the semantic roles which nouns can assume. For example, there is an agentive case corresponding to the agent of an action, an instrumental case corresponding to the object used to implement an action, a locative case, and so on.

Greenfield, Smith, and Laufer (in press) have modified Fillmore's case grammar and used this modified version to describe their longitudinal data on the holophrastic period. They stress as one advantage of this system the fact that it highlights the continuity between speech in the holophrastic and combinatorial phases of development. The relations used are:

pure performative	object of demand
vocative	locative
naming	action or state of inanimate object
action	entity associated with thing or place
inanimate object of direct action	experiencer
	agent of action
negative or affirmative	modification of event.

According to these authors, holophrases serving the above function 'do not have global meanings by themselves, but rather combine in specific, determined, structured ways with situational elements' (p. 81). Again, then, a holophrase does not represent a whole sentence to a child, but rather a specific relation which cannot be understood by adults without considering the situational context of the utterance.

There are two other formulations which have been used to describe various stages of child language and which are assumed to apply to the holophrastic period. The first is Gruber's (1967) 'topic-comment' formulation. On the basis of observations of a single child, Mackie, Gruber first suggests that Mackie's three- and four-word sentences do not seem to fit the adult subject–predicate model. Gruber proposes a process of 'topicalization' to account for such sentences as 'it broken, wheels', 'car, it broken', and 'dump truck all fixed'. Gruber suggests that the child simultaneously generates a topic, which can be either a noun or a case-marked pronoun, and a comment, which is in essence a 'subjectless sentence'. Using a series of rules, Gruber can explain the patterns of distribution in Mackie's speech, in which topics occur with about equal frequency preceding and following the comments, as well as various peculiarities of the sentences produced. Although Gruber proposed his analysis to explain a period in combinatorial speech which obviously follows the holophrastic period, he has suggested the extension of this interpretation to include single-word utterances.

This type of extension has been proposed by Antinucci and Parisi(1973), based upon the data provided by one-, two-, and three-word utterances from Claudia, an Italian monolingual, between the ages of fifteen and nineteen months. Basing their arguments on a generative semantic model, Antinucci and Parisi assume that for every surface structure which Claudia utters, there is an abstract underlying structure based upon two ideas. First, the underlying structure involves a certain number of 'complements', or words which could be expressed in the complete sentence. The number of complements actually expressed determines the length of the utterance produced. With this explanation, Antinucci and Parisi can propose the same underlying structure for a one-, two-, or three-word utterance. The difference is the number of complements expressed; in the abstract structure all complements are present. In this analysis, single-word utterances are truly 'holophrastic'; an entire sentential thought is assumed to be expressed with a single word. The second half of the formulation is again based upon Austin's (1965) notion of performative verbs, verbs such as 'I promise' which do not merely describe an action, but actually perform the action by their very utterance. Antinucci and Parisi similarly divide Claudia's speech into two functional categories: descriptive and requesting. The difference between these two categories is used to explain differences among apparently similar surface structures, as well as similarities among apparently different surface structures.

SOME EMPIRICAL AND THEORETICAL PROBLEMS IN THE STUDY OF SINGLE-WORD SPEECH

Smith (1970) and Greenfield et al. (in press) cite several obvious reasons many researchers have not attempted to analyze such early linguistic productions. The problems inherent in any observational study of early language acquisition are multiplied at this stage. In any investigation of this type, sample size must be kept small, the time needed to obtain a sizable corpus of utterances is large, and many of the utterances are open to a variety of interpretations, yielding data which are often uncertain. At the single-word stage, children speak very infrequently, their words are often unintelligible, or only marginally intelligible, and it may be very difficult to determine the proper context of an utterance. It is necessary, then, for the investigator to acquaint himself with each child in order that he may understand both the child's vocabulary, and the extralinguistic situations in which verbal production occurs. Many investigators have been unable to devote large amounts of time to this type of undertaking, and as noted, many have been reluctant to rely heavily on extralinguistic context to determine the meaning of an utterance for the child.

The issue of the empirical verifiability of linguistic structures discovered through the use of extralinguistic context has already been discussed in a previous section. Another question, however, remains. Once non-linguistic material is introduced, any resulting structural description cannot be regarded as 'linguistic' in a pure sense. For purposes of this study, the terms 'linguistic structure' and 'psycholinguistic structure' will be used loosely and interchangeably. The structures themselves are not derived from any single system described above, but rather have been devised to suit the purposes of this study. They will be described in detail in following chapters.

In summary, the literature discussed in the preceding sections indicates that there is a long precedent for the study of psycholinguistic development during the holophrastic period. There is evidence that holophrases are used in ways that are relational, that the development of holophrases is continuous with later development during the combinatorial period, and that the use of extralinguistic context is not only legitimate, but necessary for the adult's understanding of the child's use of holophrases. The evolution of the notion of a holophrase has been described, illustrating the trend away from the belief that a holophrase is an adult sentence to the current idea that a holophrase is the child's primitive means of expressing something similar to what an adult expresses in a particular type of semantic relation. It is time, then, to focus upon the relation between language acquisition during the holophrastic period and cognitive development which should be occurring at the same time.

The relation between linguistic development and cognitive development during the single-word period

Of course, language development does not begin or progress in a vacuum. The question of the relationship between language acquisition and cognitive development in general is particularly important in considering the transition from the use of holophrases to combinatorially expressed relations. The discussion of this relationship will be organized into four sections.

First, the major viewpoints are summarized, including the works of Werner and Kaplan, Vygotsky, Bruner, and Piaget. Next, Bloom's (1973) position regarding the relation between cognitive development and single-word speech in particular will be presented. Third is a discussion of possible parallels between specific psycholinguistic and cognitive skills, as such parallels will be involved in this study. Finally, the theoretical and empirical problems involved in the investigation of the relation between language acquisition and cognitive development will be discussed.[1]

Theoretical viewpoints regarding language and cognition:
Werner and Kaplan, Vygotsky, Bruner, and Piaget

All the above-mentioned authors regard human language as a symbol system which is unique to this species. Since it operates by means of symbols or things, i.e. words, which stand for other things, language necessarily depends upon representational ability. This representational ability in turn depends upon several basic skills which must have been previously acquired. The child must be aware that there are objects separate from himself, and that these objects at least to some degree are permanent and retain their identity regardless of his actions with them, and regardless of whether he can even see them at the present time. This ability also entails memory; the child must somehow be aware of the previous existence of an object which is no longer present. Although there are numerous other requisite skills and abilities, these two are perhaps the most central. None of the investigators in this field disagrees with this point. The arguments, rather, center upon how finely developed these skills and abilities must be before language development can proceed, and about the 'origin' or impetus of linguistic development. Is this an independent occurrence, or is it but one aspect of the complicated unfolding of cognitive processing skills?

Werner and Kaplan (1963) view language development, or symbol formation, as they term it, as one tightly interrelated aspect of the child's over-all development according to the 'orthogenetic principle', the continuing complementary processes of ever-increasing differentiation and integration. Symbol formation cannot occur until both cognitive and affective development have proceeded to the point where the child

---

[1] Since this book went to press, several articles and reports have appeared which reflect a change in focus in the developmental psycholinguistic literature toward increasing interest in the relationship between the child's first words and his ongoing cognitive development. These could not be reviewed here, since they were not available. (See for example, Dore, 1973; McNeill, 1974; Nelson, 1973, 1974; Sinclair, 1971.)

has differentiated himself both from his mothering figure and from the inanimate objects which surround him. Once this occurs, however, the primitive roots of symbolic ability begin to develop immediately, from a variety of sources. Early symbolic ability is intimately connected to the child's own actions. If one ignored this action-aspect of symbolism and looked only at verbal productions, he would be entirely unaware of the beginnings of the types of relations, both syntactic and semantic which form the basis for language. For example, Werner and Kaplan painstakingly trace the development of gesture, from early chance touching, through deliberate handling, reaching, and pointing to illustrate the basis for the child's first understanding of the deictic function. They point out how and why the deictic function must be well established before the child can progress to depiction, and in a similar fashion, they trace the non-verbal roots of depiction. Two of Werner and Kaplan's basic points have already been mentioned in a previous section. First, they depend heavily upon the interrelation to nonlinguistic content in explaining linguistic development. Second, their entire approach is developmental; they document specific changes in relations over each period. This is of particular interest here with respect to the holophrastic period which might at first appear to be unitary. Werner and Kaplan consider it legitimate to discuss relations with respect to the use of single words. These relations are often analogous to non-linguistic cognitive relations, and in all cases their development is dependent on previous and concurrent developments in other spheres, but they are not identical with cognitive changes and they can, at least theoretically, be discussed in isolation from them.

While Werner and Kaplan thus stress the unitary beginning of all development, and the differentiation which occurs between language and thought even at the same time the two functions are being integrated, Vygotsky (1962) is perhaps best known for the hypothesis that language and thought in man have basically independent roots. During the course of development, the two functions combine, and their fate becomes intertwined. Each undergoes further refinement, but beyond a certain point they can no longer be separated, except in the abstract. While he devotes a great deal of attention to the development of 'meaning' and 'sense', Vygotsky is not particularly interested either in the development of syntactic relations, or even in semantic relations as they influence grammar. His work is largely concerned with the intersection of language and thought, both with the process of concept formation as it evolves in young children, and with the development of various types of concepts which he postulates during later childhood and adolescence.

By far the greatest amount of attention to the types of cognitive and symbolic relations which develop during the age range in which holophrases flourish has come from the massive research efforts of Piaget and his followers. Since it would be impossible to present Piaget's entire theory of sensory-motor development here the discussion below will again concentrate on the nature of language as 'symbolic function' and its consequent relationship to cognitive development in general, and on the specific types of sensory-motor development which must precede the appearance of speech in which relations, either syntactic or semantic, can be expressed.

Sinclair-de-Zwart (1969) explains that language is only one aspect of a more general symbolic function. This function arises at the end of the sensory-motor period, about eighteen months of age, with the concurrent appearance of combinatorial speech, symbolic play, and deferred imitation. These developments have been prepared for by the development of cognitive structures up to that point on the sensory-motor level. Prior sensory-motor development is an essential prerequisite for the emergence of the symbolic function. Before the the child becomes able to internally represent objects and events in the world around him he must, through his active participation, develop a repertoire of action schemas, which in essence form a first external representation of the world through direct action and sensory experience. Development on the sensory-motor level culminates with the object concept, the child's active understanding of both object constancy and object permanence. In other words, the child has become aware that there are objects which exist external to himself, that these objects continue to exist regardless of whether he is performing any action with them or receiving sense input from them (object permanence), and that these objects retain their character regardless of the particular action the child is performing with the object (object constancy). For example, the child is by now aware that a nursing bottle exists, even when he is not sucking at it, and even when he cannot see it, and that this is the same bottle regardless of whether he is sucking milk from it or throwing it, or looking at it with the nipple up or down (Piaget, 1952, 1962). According to Piaget this object concept can only develop through the interco-ordination of action patterns, called schemas, such as the schemas for sucking, looking, throwing the bottle. In turn, the object concept is prerequisite for the emergence of representational, or symbolic ability. The appearance of this symbolic ability, evidenced by the appearance of symbolic speech, combinatorial speech, and deferred imitation is thus a logical outgrowth of the prior sensory-motor achievement.

The notion that language, or symbolic structure, is first intimately tied to actions was mentioned not only in conjunction with other cognitive theorists (Werner and Kaplan, 1963; Vygotsky, 1962; Bruner, Olver, and Greenfield, 1966) but also in the discussion of linguistic development per se (de Laguna, 1927; McNeill, 1970b; Smith, 1970; Greenfield, Smith, and Laufer, in press; Brown, 1973; Nelson, 1973). McNeill has noted that this fact is particularly compatible with Piaget's and other theories that abstract intelligence evolves from active sensory-motor intelligence. The hypothesis presented by Bruner, Olver, and Greenfield (1966) would also fit these facts. Bruner et al. accept most of Piaget's findings and formulations, but go on to claim that there are three modes of representation which appear in fixed developmental progression. The three are: enactive or sensory-motor, iconic or pictorial, and symbolic, including language as described by transformational linguists, and deferred imitation and symbolic play as described by Piaget. Since each of the succeeding modes is prepared for by the preceding ones, Bruner et al. again accept the thesis that the earliest expressions of linguistic relations have their roots in action.

The relation between language and cognitive development in Bloom's study of single-word speech

Bloom's study of her daughter, Allison, during the single-word period has already been mentioned. It will be recalled that her main point was that the child's utterances during the single-word period do not contain true linguistic structure of their own, but rather reflect changes in the child's cognitive modes of organizing his world and his experience. There can thus be development during the single-word period, but it is cognitive development, and not specifically linguistic. '... before the use of syntax in their speech children have little if any knowledge of linguistic structure' (p. 5). One type of evidence which Bloom uses is the interchangeability of word meanings to denote opposite poles of a cognitive concept, e.g. a child using 'up' for both up and down. This fact has been well documented, but the existence of cognitive confusion does not preclude the existence of linguistic structure.

In explaining Allison's single-word utterances, Bloom postulates the existence of an undifferentiated amalgam, defined in cognitive terms. For example, Allison once saw a martini being prepared for her father and remarked 'Dada'. Bloom suggests a fused cognitive notion of 'Daddy's martini'. In contrast, this author would explain such an utterance by the postulation of a possessive holophrase. It would seem that the child has indeed differentiated between the two parts of the relation, the possessor, 'Daddy' and the thing possessed, 'martini'. This position is reinforced by evidence from the present study in which a child, holding her father's freshly ironed pants said 'Daddy' several times. When she continued to be ignored, she then said 'bai', her consistent word for any piece of clothing. This alternation between the two parts of the relation indicates an awareness of both parts. To some extent, the identity of these two parts might still be fused, as Bloom claims, but this does not refute the fact that the child is able to utter them independently, and in a sequence which indicates an awareness of the linguistic as well as the cognitive relationship between them. Based upon this, as well as similar evidence, this author cannot accept Bloom's contention that the child has no understanding of linguistic structure until the appearance of syntax.

Some possible parallels between cognitive abilities and linguistic relations

There are several obvious parallels between some grammatical and semantic relations and some of the cognitive achievements which occur on the sensory-motor level. For example, a child using a stick to swat a hanging parrot toy perhaps exemplifies the relation 'I hit parrot' or subject–verb–object. It is obvious that development cannot occur on the psycholinguistic plane to the point that the child could explicitly state a relation such as 'I hit parrot' until both the physical speech-producing apparatus and the child's cognitive structures have reached a certain level of development. It is clear from the work of all the cognitive theorists discussed above that the earliest actions, or in Piaget's terms, 'circular reactions' will not suffice; it is not so clear that linguistic development does not begin until the very end of the sensory-motor period.

One method of measuring possible parallels between sensory-motor and linguistic relations has been suggested by Greenfield, Nelson, and Saltzman (1972). The task itself has not been discussed by Piaget, and although it is not an intuitively obvious parallel, it is mentioned here as the only study to date in this area. Using a set of graduated stacking cups ranging in size from 4.4 to 8.8 cm. in 1.1 cm. steps, Greenfield et al. discovered a progression in the strategies used by children aged eleven to thirty-six months of age in stacking the cups. The youngest children created pairs. The next strategy was called the 'pot' strategy; subjects placed all the cups in or on a large one, but did not order these by size. The last strategy to appear was the one demonstrated, the 'sub-assembly method'. One cup was placed inside the next larger cup, and that entire unit inside the next larger cup, and so on to completion. Successful subjects were given a sixth cup of intermediate size to insert in the proper position in the series.

Greenfield et al. claim that placing one cup inside another is analogous to lifting one cup as the 'actor' and placing it inside an 'object' cup. In the most advanced strategy the child must change his frame of reference and use the entire unit he has created as the new actor. An 'actor', of course, is one semantic type of syntactic 'subject' of a sentence. Both the validity of this analogy, and its interrelationship with the development of the process of seriation will be discussed later in this book.

There are examples from Piaget's own data which might be described as parallels to linguistic relations which develop later. Again looking at the syntactic relation of subject–verb–object, there are many illustrations which could be taken from Piaget's discussion of the development of the child's awareness of the causal relationship between means and ends. For example, Piaget stresses the example of the five- or six-month-old child during the period of secondary circular reactions pulling a chain in order to shake a rattle. This action could easily be interpreted in adult symbolic terms as 'chain shakes rattle' (actor–action–object semantic version of subject–verb–object syntactic relation). Of course, one cannot suppose that the child at this early stage could conceptualize his action in these terms, but the parallel is obvious and it remains possible that the child has some beginning, undifferentiated awareness of his action on a symbolic as well as a sensory-motor level. It is also possible that this rudimentary symbolic awareness develops concurrently with progress on the sensory-motor level. The parallels become increasingly plausible, of course, as the child approaches the age at which symbolic activity also occurs. At 8 months 20 days Jacqueline pulls on a string to obtain a cigarette case which is out of reach (Piaget, 1952). Again, this could be an actor–action–object relation; 'string pulls case'. By the time tertiary circular reactions have appeared, the examples and parallels are numerous. Lucienne (10 months 27 days) pulls on a handkerchief to get a bottle, 'handkerchief moves bottle'. Laurent at 11 months 16 days similarly uses a string to pull a red shoe-horn toward him.

Theoretical and empirical problems in investigating the relationship
between language acquisition and cognitive development

There are several difficulties involved in investigating the relationship between language acquisition and cognitive development. Some of these concern the possibility of constructing parallel relations, such as those described above, some involve the general theoretical connection between the two types of development, and some are empirical, practical issues of how one goes about studying a basically abstract question.

One problem involved in postulating parallels between language acquisition and other symbolic processes is the fact that one can never be sure whether the child is 'thinking' in symbolic terms at all, in addition to his concrete actions, let alone in the same fashion as an adult.

A second problem related specifically to Piaget's theory of cognitive development is this problem of inference from observable action, and the verification of such inference will by definition always be a major hazard in the scientific study of children who do not yet share the adult symbolic system. Observers see only the child's various actions, e.g. pulling a string to bring an object within reach, or opening and closing one's mouth when confronted with the problem of widening the opening in a matchbox, followed by the child's then enlarging the opening (Piaget, 1952). Any interpretation which claims that these actions demonstrate the emergence of processes of abstraction and symbolism is, of course, an assumption on the part of the adult observer, or more accurately, an analogy between what the child has done, and the processes by which an adult would co-ordinate a similar series of actions. Such inferences are useful when they reveal regularities and progressions in the child's actions, and his symbolic and communicative abilities. It must be stressed repeatedly, however, that to some degree the regularities apparent to adults are revealed because the adults themselves share a symbolic system which produces these regularities. The only direct means of verification of the child's usage of the same symbolic processes would be to ask the child to describe his understanding of the world in symbolic terms, and, of course, a child who has not yet acquired the complex system of communication, syntax, semantics, and cognitive abilities which comprises the shared language in use around him is unable to do this! To overcome this inherent obstacle, investigators must rely on the regularities revealed through second-hand observation by adults. This type of study is a legitimate scientific tool in measuring the child's progress as long as investigators are aware that, at best, they are producing a working model of the child's development in the symbolic sphere. Such a model, if it describes the data accurately, can provide much valuable information without necessarily being 'psychologically real' in the mind of the child. Particular models can be selected and eliminated as more or less appropriate in terms of the total situation. For example, one way to conceive of the problem of language acquisition and symbolic process in general is that, from the child's point of view, he must first become aware that such systems exist and are in use around him, and then he must discover and apply the various hierarchies of rules which govern these systems. Since it is known that the endpoint of this development is the emergence of a system like that used by adults around him, it is logical to assume that this adult system is influencing the ongoing course of development, and that much of the child's early actions and symbolic attempts can be interpreted as approximations to this same adult system. The larger question of just how much inference from observable data is legitimate, and where one draws the line between the pre-symbolic and the symbolic child are much more difficult to answer, and may depend, in the last analysis on the theoretical predilections of the investigators.

Piaget and his co-workers are not particularly concerned with relations within the symbolic function. They are interested particularly in the conditions which permit development of the symbolic function, including language, but not with the technicalities of grammar and semantics within language once it has appeared. Similarly, they are concerned with the conditions giving rise to the separation of the permanent object, but not with the later fate of the agent—object relationship as it is discussed in linguistics and psycholinguistics. Nevertheless, it is important to demonstrate through this type of relation that Piaget's theories are not inherently contradictory to the work of American developmental psycholinguistics. This misconception has led many investigators to believe that one cannot accept both the work of Piaget and the work of the developmental psycholinguists; it is time for this notion to be dispelled.

Piaget claims that before the permanent object has been established the child often behaves in ways which suggest that he is using this concept, but that this behavior is misleading. Instead, the object is fused with the particular action schema which the child is exercising, and it is this schema as a whole that the child 'remembers' on an action level. All of Piaget's evidence in favor of this point (of course, this is another example of theoretical inference from observable behavior) does not rule out the possibility that the child at this stage might also be capable of utilizing linguistic relations, probably in an equally primitive form. Just as there may be cognitive amalgams which develop into adult skills, so there might be linguistic skills which develop, and it may be useful to describe them in adult terms while remembering that the child is yet using them in an early, undifferentiated form.

There are several related issues involved. First, it has clearly been shown by many cognitive theorists that there is much development on the action plane, or sensory-motor level, before combinatorial speech appears. As stated, this does not imply that there has been no development on a more specifically psycholinguistic level. Second, although some degree of cognitive sophistication in sensory-motor terms is necessary before the child can employ linguistic relations, Piaget never claims that he must progress all the way to representational intelligence, so this is not an issue. Third, although it is true that approximately eighteen months of sensory-motor development invariably precede the appearance of combinatorial speech, the temporal sequence does not imply causality. Fourth, as noted several times, no previous investigator of holophrastic speech has claimed that the 'sentence' or the 'relation' which the child was expressing with a holophrase was understood by the child in the same detailed fashion as by an adult. The types of vague, global intent to express something like a sentence or a grammatical relation have been discussed in detail above and will not be repeated here. If holophrastic language is conceived in this way, and if language acquisition consists of the child's increasing ability to differentiate a global 'sentence' into its component relations and parts, and to achieve a clearer understanding of each part as well as of the inter-relationship of parts, then there is no longer any inconsistency with Piaget's data. There is no reason, for example, that a child must completely under-stand object permanency in Piaget's sense in order to refer to an object in a particular situation. Smith's previously mentioned example in which 'fan' and 'on' both express the same relation, 'I want the fan on', might be cited in support of this interpretation.

Sinclair-de-Zwart (1969) objects to the postulation of innate gram-matical relations (McNeill, 1966) which do not develop from previous sensory-motor structures. This, however, no longer appears to be an issue. As illustrated above, it is compatible with the work of Piaget and Sinclair-de-Zwart that psycholinguistic structures are undergoing initial develop-ment during the sensory-motor period; the question of comparative rate remains open. There is no reason why, even before the full achievement of representational intelligence, there could not be a fleeting, situation-bound symbol which could be involved in a relation, corresponding perhaps to the fleeting action-bound object described by Piaget. Both Werner and Kaplan (1963) and Vygotsky (1962) mention such ill-defined precursors to true symbols as essential to symbolic development.

Before concluding, there is one issue which has been raised above which has not been dealt with completely. This is the question of whether the child interprets the adult's actions and words in the same manner as an adult. Again, since one cannot ask the child for his interpretation, investigators must rely on inferences from behavior. All of the evidence cited above would suggest that the child does not share the adult interpretation. On the linguistic level, there has been one study dealing with the related issue of whether children respond maximally to material presented 'at their own level' or in adult form. Shipley, Smith, and Gleitman (1969) attempted to determine whether children are more likely to obey commands phrased in child-like or adult language. All the commands involved interaction with attractive toys; the children ranged from eighteen to thirty-three months of age. Only the four youngest children preferred the simplified forms; the general trend was for children to obey commands presented in complete, correct English. Although one cannot assume from this evidence that the children interpreted the 'adult' forms in an adult manner, it is apparently not detrimental to use adult forms in conversation with children, and consequently not inappropriate to use adult comparisons, with reservation, in describing children's utterances.

In summary, the literature described above provides some evidence that the development of holophrases is continuous not only with later linguistic development during the combinatorial period, but also with previous cognitive development on the action level. The relation to previous sensory-motor development has been described in detail, with respect not only to the work of Piaget, but other cognitive theorists as well. It was concluded that although an unknown amount of sensory-motor development is prerequisite to the use of symbolic relations as found during psycholinguistic development, there is nothing in Piaget's theory which is incompatible with the early development of grammatical and semantic relations during the sensory-motor period.

2 The present research as it relates to earlier work

It has been shown in chapter 1 that many previous investigators have believed that there is a 'holophrastic period', during the normal course of language acquisition, i.e. a period in which a child uses a single-word utterance to express something similar to the meaning which adults convey through the use of a relation, such as Fillmore's case relations (see Greenfield et al., in press) which involve more than one word. Some investigators have even attributed to the holophrase the meaning conveyed by an entire adult sentence. Previous studies have also provided evidence that from the onset of the holophrastic period, at about the age of twelve months, until the appearance of combinatorial speech, at about the age of eighteen months, the use of holophrases undergoes considerable development. In light of these considerations, this research was designed to have three major goals. The first goal is to document the usage of holophrastic or relational single-word speech in a substantial number of children. The second is to demonstrate continuity in three linguistic relations from the end of the holophrastic period into the beginnings of the combinatorial period. The third is to provide some insight into the relationship between linguistic and cognitive abilities at the end of the holophrastic period which, of course, coincides roughly with the end of Piaget's sensory-motor period.

In order to study the first problem, a series of observation sessions was included as the first phase of the study. The purpose of these sessions was to collect a corpus of utterances from each child in the study. These utterances were to be analyzed as holophrastic speech, in order to demonstrate that such an analysis was feasible, and at the same time to provide comparable data on single-word speech produced by a sizable number of children which could be compared to reveal patterns of holophrastic usage across children. Further, such patterns, indicating which linguistic relations were being expressed holophrastically by each child, were essential for the second part of the study. Phase two consisted of a training program aimed at three linguistic relations; subject–verb–object, possessive, and locative which can be expressed holophrastically, and through combinatorial speech. The goal of this program was to train two-word expression of relations which were already being used holophrastically.

Finally, in order to study the third question, sensory-motor tasks were designed which could be conceived of as cognitive 'correlates' to some of these linguistic relations. Children's performance on the linguistic and sensory-motor correlates was to be compared in order to determine whether there was indeed a prerequisite level of cognitive skill required before a relation could be expressed in the linguistic medium. Before the method actually used can be described, however, there are several theoretical questions which remain to be clarified.

The first issue is the exact definition of a holophrase. The definition presented in chapter 1 will be repeated here. As employed in this study, the *term holophrase refers to a single-word utterance which is used by a child to express more than the meaning usually attributed to that single word by adults.* A holophrase does not necessarily, however, convey the meaning of an entire adult sentence. Rather, it conveys a consistent linguistic relation, which might or might not comprise an entire sentence. For example, a holophrastic utterance embodying the subject—verb—object relation might easily be glossed by a complete sentence, e.g. 'hit' as in 'Mommy *hit* the doll'. A holophrase indicating possession, such as 'Daddy' referring to '*Daddy*'s pants', on the other hand, would gloss as only part of an adult sentence. For purposes of this study, any consistent system of relations could be used in glossing holophrases. This would include the semantic system proposed by Smith (1970) which is based largely on the adult's interpretation of the child's intention in uttering the holophrase, Fillmore's case-grammar relations as modified by Greenfield, Smith, and Laufer (in press), the syntactic relations described by McNeill (1966, 1970a, 1970b) as well as any of the other systems of relations described in chapter 1.

The current study was performed before the Greenfield et al. (in press) results were available. The three relations studied – subject—verb—object, possessives, and locatives – were chosen not for their theoretical position in any particular system of linguistic relations, but because it appeared from the author's preliminary observations and from Smith's (1970) data that these three would enable one to study a range of individual differences among children during the holophrastic period. All three had been noted to appear holophrastically in at least some children, but all three were not usually used by the same child at the same time. This would allow the selection of children who were using some, but not all of the relations holophrastically at the onset of the study. Further, since all three of these relations were known to appear early in combinatorial speech, they were a logical choice for a study investigating continuity between the holophrastic and two-word periods. Other relations mentioned, but not specifically selected for this study, were similarly classified. For example, all instances of 'no' or 'not' were classed as negative holophrases. The classification of all possible holophrases into sub-types such as negatives of rejection was beyond the scope of this study, just as the requirement that all the 'relations' described be previously considered to be part of the same system of analysis was considered to be begging the question. If one could begin with the child's holophrastic utterances and create a system of relations, then one could conclude that structure did exist within holophrastic usage. The question is answered, then, not by fitting templates in the form of 'systems of relations' to the data, but by working from the data to an appropriate system. Some other relations which were classified as holophrastic usage in this study were 'salutes' such as 'hi' and 'bye' to use Roger Brown's term, 'attributives' such as 'hot', 'pretty', or 'white' which were always adjectives which described the properties of nouns, and 'where-holophrases' a specific type of interrogative which were literally the child's utterance of 'where' when the non-linguistic context clearly indicated that he was asking a question of the type '*Where* is the ———?' or '*Where* did the ——— go?' Some of these could be accommodated reasonably well by a description of syntactic 'relations' from transformational grammar; others could not. An example of the latter category is the 'I want' holophrase, as described by Smith (1970); this is a semantic classification in which the child makes his desires known. He does not say 'I want' but rather a single word describing the action or object desired, e.g. 'doll' as in 'I want the *doll*', 'ride' as in 'I want to *ride* the horse', or 'up' as in 'I want to get *up*.' Three different parts of speech are uttered, yet the underlying relation is assumed to be the same.

Since this study included a training program, the goal of which was to teach a child to express in a two-word utterance a relation which he was already expressing by means of a single-word, or holophrastic utterance, the second theoretical issue involves the conditions under which it should or should not be possible successfully to conduct such training. Both Piaget (1952 and elsewhere) and Sinclair-de-Zwart (1969, 1970, no date) would claim that a training program dealing with specifically linguistic material should be unsuccessful for two reasons. First, both would claim that the linguistic training program would be ineffective until most of the achievements of the sensory-motor period had been attained. After that time, the results of such a program would be gratuitous since linguistic development would unfold as a direct outgrowth of sensory-motor achievement, and it would be impossible to separate the effects of training from the effects of sensory-motor learning. This would suggest that the most effective way to 'train' linguistic achievement would be to improve general cognitive ability on the sensory-motor level, so that language acquisition would naturally follow. Other cognitive theorists, such as Werner and Kaplan (1963) might be more amenable to the notion of direct training, since they discuss the reciprocal effects of experience on the action and symbolic levels. They, however, would probably be pessimistic about the effects of training in general since development is a rather determined process from the outset. This question is directly relevant to McNeill's (1970) discussion of weak linguistic universals, universal linguistic abilities which are rooted in more general universal cognitive abilities. McNeill points out that a correlation in temporal sequence does not necessarily imply that the cognitive achievement was necessary and sufficient for the appearance of a universal psycholinguistic achievement. On her part, Sinclair-de-Zwart believes that cognitive development is necessary, although perhaps not sufficient.

Piaget and Sinclair-de-Zwart have a second objection to this type of study, which is shared by other cognitive theorists. They believe that stable levels of cognitive achievement are attained only through the refinement and interco-ordination of many existing schemata. According to this viewpoint, a short-term training program can provide little more than a temporary and unstable grasp of a new concept. A child may verbalize a concept correctly, yet not understand its full ramifications, and should be unable to generalize it and to apply it in all possible situations. This possibility can be precluded, however, by including tests of retention and generalization as part of any training program. Theoretically, it is of utmost importance in demonstrating continuity in psycholinguistic development that the relations trained can be demonstrated to be an integrated part of each child's linguistic competence. If it can be shown that such relations are not situation-bound, but are stable and generalizable, then the above objection will have been met. As for the larger questions of permanence of training effects in the long term, and the effect which training has on the rate and pattern of further development, these are beyond the scope of this study. This is not an intervention program aimed at accelerating development, but rather a manipulation with the aim of demonstrating continuity. If training should prove successful, of course, the possibility of intervention in language acquisition, particularly in cases of language delay, would remain to be examined.

Concluding, then, that appropriately designed training programs are viable in general, the question narrows to training of psycholinguistic relations, and specifically holophrastic utterances. None of the authors mentioned in chapter 1 has discussed the trainability of the early expression of relations. There is no reason apparent from any of the theoretical work at this early stage that such an attempt should not be made. With respect to the question of which relations could be trained and which could not, one would logically hypothesize that it should be possible to train a child to express in two words a relation which he was already expressing holophrastically while it should be more difficult, if not impossible, to train into two-word expression a relation which has never been used in a single-word utterance.

Of course, several implicit assumptions are involved. The first is that through training it will be possible to overcome whatever limitations have confined the child to the use of single words. The second is that this use of single words is not a result of situational factors, but truly results from the current state of the child's underlying linguistic competence, i.e. his knowledge of his native language. At this point, competence would include an awareness of relationships, but not yet include the ability to differentiate out either the components of the relations or the nuances involved. This in turn implies that while training in differentiation should be possible, it is very important to identify correctly the relations which are salient to a particular child. It is clear from previous investigations that marked individual differences exist among the relations expressed by children. Bloom (1970) has noted that at the early two-word stage, one child was using a pivot-open type of grammar, while two others used grammars with rules much closer to adult syntax. Brown (1973) also notes that pivot-open grammars were apparently appropriate for three children in Braine's study (see Braine, 1963), while very different grammars were required for the three children in his own longitudinal study (see Brown, Bellugi, and Cazden, 1968). Smith (1970) was able to classify major types of holophrastic sentences for three children. Although he found an invariant order of appearance of these major types, he included a large category of 'other' holophrases which varied greatly in content and order of appearance from child to child; this category included the three relations – subject–verb–object, possessives, and locatives – considered in this study. Greenfield et al. (in press) found corresponding differences between two children from Smith's study when they re-classified the data according to a case-grammar system. Although Nelson's (1973) data were not available at the time that this investigation was being planned, she, too has stressed the different types of words used by different children, and the apparent stylistic variation in language acquisition.

It is also possible that there is some non-psycholinguistic neurological or physiological mechanism which must develop before the child can begin to produce two-word utterances. One possibility suggested by McNeill (1971) is a mechanism for imposing serial order upon the words in a sentence, such as that proposed by Lashley (1951). If the child were unable to combine two words without such a mechanism, then no amount of training in which words to combine would be of any help.

Considering all the above, a training program as described would provide clear-cut evidence for continuity in the specific development of grammatical relations from the holophrastic period onward, if the following conditions were met:

1. A large proportion of single-word utterances sampled can be classified as examples of holophrastic relations.

2. Training in expressing relations in two-word utterances is successful in the case of relations which the child had been expressing holophrastically, and unsuccessful in other cases.

3. Relations which are successfully trained are retained over an interim period, and are generalizable to new situations.

Other results, not quite so clear-cut would also be explainable. If all three relations were trainable, even though one was not expressed holophrastically, there could be two compatible explanations. First, it is possible that the subject was holophrastically expressing all these relations, but that no examples of some relations appeared in the recorded sample. The presence of an observer and a tape recorder might contribute to the inhibition of ordinary speech production. Alternately, it is possible that while certain relations were not yet expressed, the child had the capacity, either innate or recently acquired, to do so, i.e. the relation chronologically enters competence before it appears in performance. Such an assertion, of course, is extremely difficult to disprove empirically.

The problem is more complicated if no relation should prove trainable, whether or not it was expressed holophrastically. The most obvious conclusion is that the training is inappropriate, and perhaps the failure of this particular procedure says nothing about the trainability of relations in general. Again, this argument is unanswerable. The only comment appropriate here is that training procedures must be carefully designed not only to be well-suited to the expression of a particular type of relation, but to accommodate the past history and performance of each child. Special precautions must be taken to make materials interesting to children of this age, and to adjust for such variables as short attention span.

Another set of theoretical problems arises in connection with the second goal of the study, to provide some insight into the relationship between linguistic and cognitive abilities at the end of the holophrastic period. The method chosen was to devise 'correlate' sensory-motor or cognitive relations to the linguistic relations, as well as to measure some of Piaget's established hallmarks of sensory-motor achievement. The first questions, then, are whether it is possible to devise such correlates, and if so, how one decides whether the linguistic and cognitive tasks chosen truly are correlates.

The question of whether it is possible to devise such correlates can probably never be answered to the satisfaction of all concerned. Again, this is because it is impossible to determine whether the child is using a correlate, or conceptualizes in the same terms as the adult who describes it. In fact, the bulk of Piaget's work, as well as that of Werner and Kaplan (1963) illustrates precisely the point that the child's mode of thought is basically different from that of the adult. Psycholinguists acknowledge the same point with respect to linguistic development when they ascribe different grammars to children and to adults. In order to answer this question at all, one must be willing to divide it into two sections. First, is it useful for adults to treat cognitive development and language development as if such correlates exist? The answer, already discussed in chapter 1, is obviously yes, since such treatment points out the regularities and similarities between the two spheres. Second, is there any reason to assume that at least on some level, the child makes a connection in his mind between similar cognitive and linguistic processes? The evidence which Werner and Kaplan (1963) provide would indicate that the answer to this question is also yes. Precursors to symbol formation are being employed by the child at precisely the same time in which cognitive functions are forming; one would expect the two processes mutually to influence one another. Also, the mere fact that the action-oriented and symbolic expressions eventually fuse would lead one to believe that the child begins at an early age to establish primitive, ill-defined connections between the two which he can only understand as the two functions become progressively refined. All of this, of course, is hypothetical, but it is at least as plausible to assume from the data that the child makes some primitive connection as to assume that he does not. Finally, the possibility remains that there is no distinction between language and thought processes, but very few persons would make such an extreme claim.

The question of how to choose correlates is even more complicated. At this early stage in the investigation of this area, the only way to proceed is by theoretically guided trial-and-error. The best one can do is to try to find cognitive tasks which appear, at least to an adult, to parallel linguistic relations, and then to design an investigation which will determine whether the connection really exists. As mentioned in chapter 1, only one previous investigation (Greenfield et al., 1972) has been concerned with this attempt; the relation involved was agent–action–object, one semantic aspect of the syntactic subject–verb–object relation included in this study and the correlate was the strategy used by a child in arranging seriated stacking cups. An adaptation of this task was included in the present investigation. The other correlates used will be described in detail below, the results will be presented in chapter 4, and the theoretical problems with each correlate will be discussed in chapter 5.

The justification for a second correlate of the subject–verb–object relationship has already been presented in chapter 1. As mentioned, this involves the means-end relation and can be illustrated as follows. Jacqueline at 9 months 8 days (Piaget, 1952) uses a doll attached at one end of a string to shake a toy parrot. One can imagine the relation

doll	shakes	parrot
(subject)	(verb)	(object)

or even the more complicated relation

I	shake	doll
	doll	shakes	parrot

in which the doll, which is first the object of an action, becomes immediately the actor and the syntactic subject in a second action.

The correlate devised to parallel the locative relation, the ability to say where something is located, is the active ability to find it. Piaget (1952) describes advances in the child's ability to retrieve an object which has undergone a series of visible and invisible displacements. The highest achievement, the retrieval of an object which has undergone two invisible displacements, occurs at the end of the sensory-motor period, or about eighteen months of age. This ability was chosen as a correlate because of its obvious connection to the linguistic skill, and also because it has been so well documented by Piaget and many others. Probably, only the first step in this series is necessary to establish a correlate ability; the entire series was included to provide additional information about sensory-motor ability. No correlate to the possessive relation was included because a suitable one could not be devised.

The other skills chosen to measure sensory-motor achievement in general were symbolic play, role playing and deferred imitation. Symbolic play and deferred imitation require no justification since they have been so well documented by Piaget, and are indeed his own hallmarks for the completion of sensory-motor development. Role playing ability does not fully develop until much later, but its roots are found during the sensory-motor period. The particular tasks chosen to represent these skills will be described in chapter 3.

The remaining theoretical issues, then, center around the question of how one knows, once sensory-motor skills, and measured changes over time in psycholinguistic development have been tested, what the relationship is between these cognitive and psycholinguistic skills. There are many outcomes to consider. If all subjects show advanced development in both spheres, the study has essentially provided no new information. If all children appear to have completed sensory-motor development, yet show marked differences in psycholinguistic abilities, one would infer although not conclusively, both that sensory-motor development precedes linguistic development in temporal sequence if not in causal relationship, and also that the acquisition of a cognitive skill does not imply the acquisition of a corresponding linguistic skill. This type of result would cause one to wonder whether the linguistic and cognitive skills truly were correlates. If, on the other hand, training in psycholinguistic relations was successful for one or both relations, but a child did not show evidence of having completed sensory-motor development, this would imply that linguistic relations are learned independently of sensory-motor relationships, and do not depend upon the appearance of a unified 'symbolic function' as Piaget describes it. Strictly speaking, from the Piagetian viewpoint, the close of the sensory-motor period signals the advent of representational intelligence, so that no relational use of language should occur before that time. The possibility of amalgams of psycholinguistic relations, or undifferentiated precursors to psycholinguistic relations has already been discussed in detail in chapter 1, and will not be repeated here. Essentially, the introduction of this possibility eliminates any disagreement with Piaget's system.

Finally, there remains the possibility of mixed results. Some children may begin functioning at an advanced level on some cognitive tasks, yet show primitive action levels on other tasks. Unless the discrepancy is striking, however, it is not a major problem. Piaget includes in his system the possibility of décalage, or the repetition of similar processes of development at different times for different tasks. Werner and Kaplan (1963) describe an essentially similar property as the 'spirality' of cognitive development. Bruner et al. (1966) also mention the persistence of primitive modes of thought even after more advanced modes have begun to evolve. Mixed results might somewhat weaken Sinclair-de-Zwart's claim that simultaneity of onset is a source of evidence for the unity of the symbolic function, but they would not essentially do any damage to the major tenets of any of the cognitive systems.

Having dealt with the theoretical issues which inspired this study, and the theoretical questions raised by its design, it is time to turn to a description of the design and the method as used.

3 Design and procedures for the present study

SUBJECTS

Ten subjects were selected on the basis of their level of psycholinguistic ability, as determined by mothers' reports and the experimenter's preliminary observations. At the time of their first formal observation, subjects ranged in age from 16 months 3 days to 21 months 11 days. Three male and seven female subjects were included in the study. Age and sex of subjects is shown in table 1. All subjects had been producing single-word utterances for several months. None of the subjects were known to be producing combinatorial two-word utterances, although some were using such pseudo-combinations as 'happy birthday' and 'all gone'. In a few cases, mothers reported that subjects had correctly said 'hi' or 'bye' followed by a person's name. One subject had been producing the minimum number of ten recognizable words, but all others had initial vocabularies ranging from about twenty-five to fifty words. This included words idiosyncratic to the subject

TABLE 1 *Schedule of observation, training, and follow-up sessions for the ten subjects*

S	Sex	Birth date	Age at session 1	Date, session 1	Number obs. sessions	Date of first training	Number training sessions	Delay to follow-up	Date of follow-up
Lia	F	18 Jan. 70	16–19	27 May 71	4	3 June 71	6	4 days	14 June 71
Deanna	F	23 Oct. 69	19–26	10 June 71	5	17 June 71	5	6 days	29 June 71
Glynis	F	15 Jan. 70	16–23	7 June 71	4	14 June 71	5	4 days	21 June 71
Katie	F	13 Feb. 70	16–7	21 June 71	4	2 July 71	5	3 days	15 July 71
Jordan	M	10 Sept. 69	21–11	21 June 71	5	1 July 71	5	3 days	12 July 71
Jessica	F	31 Jan. 70	16–3[a]	2 June 71	4	2 July 71	5	3 days	12 July 71
Andrew	M	13 Jan. 70	16–29	30 June 71	4	7 July 71	5	5 days	19 July 71
Ricky	M	20 Jan. 70	17–23	12 July 71	3[b]	19 July 71	5	5 days	2 Aug. 71
Paula	F	30 Dec. 69	18–17	16 July 71	4	22 July 71	5	5 days	2 Aug. 71
Felice	F	30 Jan. 70	17–20	19 July 71	4	23 July 71	5	4 days	3 Aug. 71

[a] Jessica was first observed at age 16–2. Second observation was delayed until age 16–29; the study then proceeded as usual.
[b] Ricky's three observation sessions were 1½ hours long, instead of 1 hour.

which were consistent in meaning and well known to the subject's mother.

All ten subjects came from intact white families. Nine were from upper middle-class and one from working-class background. Seven subjects were first-born children.

PROCEDURE

The study was comprised of four parts: an initial observation period to determine which relations each subject was expressing holophrastically, a series of tests of sensory-motor correlates interspersed through the observation sessions, a training period to teach the child to express in two-word utterances the relations he was already expressing in single-word utterances, and finally a follow-up session to determine whether each subject had retained and/or generalized the results of training.

THE OBSERVATION PERIOD

Each subject was observed in his home to determine which relations he was expressing holophrastically. This period was also useful in familiarizing the subject with the experimenter and the tape recorder. All subjects except one, Katie, adjusted to the situation immediately. All sessions were tape-recorded and included detailed notes on the context of each utterance. Sample transcripts showing these notes appear in appendix A. The number of observation sessions for each subject is shown in table 1. Sessions occurred on consecutive days, whenever possible. At most, the observation period extended over ten days. Each subject received a total of about four hours' observation time. If on any day the subject could not tolerate an hour of observation, the session was shortened and the next session correspondingly lengthened to achieve the four hour total. One subject, Jessica, was determined by the experimenter not to be ready for this study after one hour of observation, and observation was resumed about one month later. In nine cases, both observation and training were conducted in the subject's home, with the subject's mother present. In the tenth case, Deanna, observation and training occurred at the home of an aunt who was the child's usual baby-sitter while her mother worked. The final session for this subject was conducted in her own home, with another familiar aunt present.

The tape-recordings of the observation sessions were transcribed at the conclusion of the study. Extralinguistic context, as recorded in the experimenter's notes, was used in the interpretation and classification of single-word utterances. Each utterance was first determined to be holophrastic or non-holophrastic, in the sense described in chapter 2, and then placed in one of the categories listed below. The justification for the classification of holophrastic utterances was given in chapter 2. Categories used were:

1. Holophrastic utterances
   a. subject—verb—object — any of the three parts of this relation might have been the word actually uttered
   b. locative — both nouns and adverbs of location appeared in this category
   c. possessive — the category consisted almost exclusively of nouns naming owners of certain materials, but a few possessive pronouns did appear; there were some instances of expression of the thing possessed
   d. 'I want' — this category included utterances of the type, 'I want——' and 'I want to ——', in which the missing word is the word actually uttered
   e. negative — this includes all holophrastic utterances of negatives, mostly no or not
   f. 'Where' — 'Where' or the missing noun is the word actually uttered, as in '*Where* is the ——?' and '*Where* did the —— go?'
   g. attributive — this category includes attributive adjectives
   h. 'hi-bye' — this category consists of 'salutes' in Roger Brown's sense
   i. 'Other' — this category includes all utterances which, through the use of extralinguistic context appeared to be holophrastic and which could be considered to be examples of linguistic relations of the types described in chapter 1, but which did not appear in sufficient quantity to warrant separate categories; some common examples were 'moo' uttered while looking at a picture of a cow, as in 'The cow goes *moo*' and 'door' uttered while holding a key, as in 'Keys are for opening the *door*.'

2. Non-holophrastic utterances
   a. naming — all nouns for which there was no clear referent, and no obvious action with which their utterance could have been associated, were classified here
   b. repetition — immediate repetition of an adult's or other child's utterance. 'Repetitions' preceded by intervening conversation were classified elsewhere whenever possible
   c. 'other' — all remaining utterances, for which it was impossible for

an adult to determine a gloss, utilizing extralinguistic context, were placed in this 'waste basket' category

Some examples of the way in which extralinguistic context was used in the classification of subject–verb–object utterances should be useful, not only in demonstrating the classification procedure, but also in distinguishing the subject–verb–object category from simple naming. One situation common for Lia occurred when trains passed by her house: she could see them through a picture window. Lia's word for train was 'dai'. Often, Lia did not say anything as the train passed, but as soon as the train stopped, she said 'dai'. This was interpreted as an expression of 'train', in the subject-verb relation '*train* stopped'. A good example of the utterance of an object–noun was Deanna's utterance of 'key' as the experimenter dropped one; the relation is 'Maris dropped the *key*.' Of course, the relation could also be '*Key* dropped'. The role of the noun in the sentence, i.e. subject and object, is different, but since the relation – subject–verb–object – remains the same, this difference is not considered important.

Simple naming, in contrast to subject–verb–object expression, occurred when a subject uttered a noun which might or might not be present but which was not involved in any action and which had no apparent contextual connection. Deanna, for example, said 'bus' and 'car' when neither was present. Her aunt asked her whether she wanted to go away in a car, but she said 'no', so this was not an 'I want' utterance. The 'I want' possibility was always considered before an utterance was classified as simple naming, especially in the case of utterances such as 'book' or 'doll'.

In addition to the classification described above, the following types of utterances were also tallied:

1. Sequences of holophrases, i.e. two or more holophrastic utterances which would have appeared to be combinatorial, except for an overly large gap in time between the two utterances. These were further separated into sequences which exemplified linguistic relations, such as 'Daddy' (pause) 'pants', glossed as 'Daddy's pants', and those which did not, such as 'Mommy Daddy' for which no gloss was apparent. Classification as a sequence was based upon the time interval between words and on intonation patterns.

2. Separated sequences of holophrases. The criterion for classification was the same as for sequences; the difference was that the two segments of the sequence were separated by something which an adult said, e.g.:

Subject: more
>   Experimenter: I can't hear you.
Subject: milk

Sequences separated by extremely long time intervals, but no intervening conversation were also classified here.

3. Relational responses to questions. This category is self-explanatory, e.g.:

>   Experimenter: What is open?
>   Subject: purse

Not all answers to all questions were considered to be relational.

4. Combinations of meaningful sounds with non-meaningful words. Three classes of non-meaningful sounds were considered: 'mm', the schwa sound 'uh', and all other sounds considered together. Combinations in which the sound preceded the word and those in which the sound followed the word were both tallied.

5. Combinatorial speech. Any instances of combinatorial speech were recorded and classified as relational or non-relational, according to the same criteria used for classification of sequences of holophrases. Examples of combinations classed as relational were 'open box' and 'big car'. An example of a combination classed as non-relational is 'ju white shu bear'. Utterances such as 'happy birthday', and 'thank you' were considered to have been learned as a unit, and therefore were not classified as combinations, unless the child was also using at least one of the elements separately.

A careful record of all utterances which might be holophrastic expressions of the three target relations – subject–verb–object, locative and possessive – was kept for each subject.

It was this record which was used to determine which relations a subject was expressing holophrastically at the close of the observation period. The classification system described above was used in analyzing data from all three 'linguistic' portions of the study: observation, training, and follow-up.

TESTS OF SENSORY-MOTOR DEVELOPMENT

Two kinds of tests of sensory-motor development were given to each subject. The first tested the level of development in the cognitive correlates of linguistic relations. The second tested whether the child had reached the level of representational thought. The justification for these tests is presented in chapter 2. The tests were distributed throughout the four hours of initial observation. In this way, it was not necessary to keep the subject's attention for more than a few minutes at a time. Nevertheless, it was at times difficult to maintain the subject's interest in the task. Hence, the number of trials on each test varied from subject to subject. The actual number of trials for each subject on each test is shown in the table presenting the results for each test. On all tests the procedure was the same. The experimenter demonstrated the task to a subject and encouraged the subject to perform it. This procedure was repeated until the subject successfully performed the task three times, or until the subject refused to perform any more. No reinforcement, except the experimenter's occasional encouragement in the form of 'good', or 'You're doing fine' was used.

Tests of cognitive correlates of linguistic relations

Two cognitive correlates of the subject–verb–object relation were used:

a. The first correlate of the subject–verb–object relation is the ability to use one object to perform an action on another. This relation has been semantically described by some linguists, e.g. Fillmore, as an instrument relation. Two sets of objects were used: toy trucks and cars of different colors, and toy balls and beads of different colors. The task had two parts. First, following the experimenter's demonstration the subject must use one car or truck to push a different colored car across the table. The correlate linguistic relation is:

truck	pushes	car
(subject)	(verb)	(object)

If the subject is successful on this portion of the task, the task is reversed, so that the subject-toy becomes the object-toy. Following the experimenter's demonstration, the subject must now use the second toy to push the first. The procedure is similar with the second set of toys. First, the subject must use one ball or bead to slide another ball or bead through a tube. Then he must reverse the process. Some actions which were not scored as examples of the subject–verb–object relation were moving both toys together so they meet, moving only one toy, and moving both toys in opposite directions.

b. The second correlate of the subject–verb–object relation is a modification of the stacking cups task used by Greenfield et al. (1972) and described in chapter 1. Greenfield et al. had been concerned with the process of seriation as well as with cognitive–psycholinguistic correlates; most of the elegant features of the design which pertained to seriation were eliminated for practical reasons. As standard procedure, all the subjects sat across from the experimenter either on the floor or on a chair at a table according to the subject's own preference. In all cases, the subject's mother sat beside the subject but did not participate in any way. Each trial began with a formal demonstration by the experimenter. The experimenter first arranged the five cups in order of increasing size, always placing the smallest cup to the subject's left. The experimenter then demonstrated the most advanced strategy, always beginning with the smallest cup. The experimenter picked up the smallest cup, placed it inside the second cup and so on, until a complete five-cup structure was formed. The experimenter then unstacked the cups, replaced them in their original position, and encouraged a subject, 'Now you try it' or 'Now you do it.' If, after repeated urging, the subject did not pick up a cup, the experimenter placed the smallest cup in the subject's hand. At least one structure of two-cup size was produced before a trial was terminated. A trial continued until the subject lost interest, so that the number of structures produced in any trial varied greatly for each subject; this number is shown in table 3 on page 50. Each trial began with a new demonstration, except in the few cases that a subject grabbed a cup and began spontaneously. All trials were included in scoring. Although a maximum of six trials was expected, in one case, a spontaneous seventh trial was included.

The cognitive correlate to the locative relation was the active ability to find an object, according to the series of displacement tasks described by Piaget (1952). A maximum of three sets of objects was used for each subject, again depending upon the subject's attention span and willingness to co-operate. Each object underwent, in sequence, one, and then two visible displacements, and then one, and then two, invisible displacements. A visible displacement is one in which the experimenter hides an object while a subject is watching, with the entire operation in full view until the object is actually hidden. An invisible displacement is one in which the experimenter hides an object, working behind a screen, so that the subject does not see where the object is being hidden. In all cases, the actual displacements were the same in the visible and invisible conditions. The three basic tasks were:

1. object–a marble
   displacements (same for visible and invisible)

  a. The experimenter takes marble from one hand and places it into
     the other.
  b. After the first displacement, the experimenter places the marble in
     an opaque cup.
2. object—a ball
   displacements (same for visible and invisible)
   a. The experimenter takes ball from one hand and places it into the
      other. The hands are reversed from the order of 1 above.
   b. The experimenter, after the first displacement, places the ball in an
      open, opaque box, with the open side at the top.
3. object — a string of beads
   displacements
   a. The experimenter places the beads in an opaque glass.
   b. After the first displacement, the experimenter places the beads
      under a pillow.
In all cases, the subject's task is to find the hidden object. A trial was
scored a success only if a subject pointed to or retrieved the object.

Testing of representational thought, or general level of sensory-motor ability

Symbolic play. Three tasks were used for each subject whenever possible.
Again, due to the subject's short attention span and willingness to participate, it was not always possible to administer all three tasks. The actual
number of tasks, as well as the spontaneous instances of symbolic play, is
shown in table 5 on page 53. Tasks used were chosen from the following list.

  1. Pretend a shoe box is a telephone. Talk.
     Variation — Pretend your hand is a telephone. Talk.
  2. Pretend a rag (or scarf) is a pillow. Sleep.
  3. Pretend your hand or top of a can is a glass. Drink.
  4. Pretend you have an imaginary key. Open a door.
  5. Pretend to cook dinner.
  6. Pretend to brush your teeth.
  7. Pretend to wash or dress yourself.
  8. Pretend to wash or dress a doll.

The tasks were administered as follows: the experimenter demonstrated,
first without any verbal explanation, and encouraged a subject 'Now you try
it.' If the subject did not comply after the first demonstration, the experi-

menter repeated the demonstration, each time including a verbal explanation. The task was terminated when the subject successfully performed three of the tests, or when the subject lost interest or refused to co-operate.

Tests for role playing. Again, an optimum of three tasks was attempted for each subject, but the same limitations of attentiveness and co-operation applied. Tasks were demonstrated and accompanied by explanation in the same manner as described above in the tests of symbolic play. Tasks were chosen from the following familiar activities:

1. Pretend you are Daddy coming home from work.
2. Pretend you are Mommy making dinner.
3. Pretend you are a little baby.
4. Pretend you are the mailman.
5. Pretend you are the maid cleaning the house.
6. Pretend you are sister (brother) going to school.

Tests for deferred imitation. Once again, an optimum of three tasks was attempted for each subject, again with the same limitations. Whenever possible, the deferred imitation task was the first task presented on a particular day. The experimenter proceeded by making sure she had the subject's attention, and then demonstrating a physical activity. The subject was requested to repeat the activity immediately; this was to insure both that the subject was motorically capable of performing the action, and that the subject had attended to the demonstration. The experimenter then cautioned 'Remember what we did now. I'm going to ask you to do that for me again later, so don't forget.' Five to fifteen minutes later, the experimenter said, 'Do you remember what we were doing before? Show me what we did'. Only an actual repetition was scored as correct. Again, all spontaneous examples of deferred imitation were also recorded; these are shown in table 7 on page 54. The tasks used were:

1. Jump up and down several times.
2. Hop on one foot several times.
3. Stamp feet several times.
4. Clap hands several times.
5. Tap head several times.
6. Hit floor or book with hands several times.

Testing schedule

The tests were distributed as evenly as possible throughout the observation sessions.

TESTING FOR FORM-PREFERENCE IN COMMANDS

One other test was administered during the observation period. This was a modification of the Shipley, Smith, and Gleitman (1969) test for preference for child-formed versus well-formed commands, described in chapter 1. It was included to determine whether these young subjects had individual differences in responsiveness to these types of verbal presentations, since both types were included in the training procedures.

Ten pairs of commands were used. Whenever possible, no two members of a pair appeared consecutively. The ten pairs were:

1.	Bounce me the ball.	Bounce ball.	(throw)
2.	Play me the music.	Play music.	
3.	Ring the bell.	Ring bell.	(shake)
4.	Roll me the marble.	Roll marble.	(bead)
5.	Open the box.	Open box.	
6.	Throw me the horseshoe.	Throw horseshoe.	
7.	Squeeze the pillow.	Squeeze pillow.	
8.	Pull me the wheelbarrow.	Pull wheelbarrow.	(wagon)
9.	Push the lawnmower.	Push lawnmower.	
10.	Break the balloon.	Break balloon.	(ball) (cup)

The words shown in parentheses were substituted in the case of the subjects who were not familiar with a word in the basic list, and in the case of temporary unavailability of one of the objects. In all cases, the experimenter merely stated the command, and waited for the subject to respond. For scoring purposes, the subject must actually perform some action with the object which was close to the action requested; gestures and glances were not scored, since this may have indicated attention to the name of the object only, rather than to the command. Because of the length of this task, it was occasionally administered in two parts to accommodate the subject's short attention span.

THE TRAINING PROGRAM

The training program began as soon as possible after observation and testing were completed. All subjects understood their own names, but rarely used them. All subjects understood the experimenter's name, Maris, but only two, Andrew and Felice, used it. All subjects used some word for their mothers' names.

The length of each training session depended upon the subject's attention span. Training continued for five consecutive days, excluding weekends and holidays. One subject, Lia, had a sixth training session. In one case, Ricky, training was interpreted for five days because the subject had roseola. Sessions usually lasted about one-and-a-half hours. As noted, except in the case of Deanna and her aunt, the subject's mother was present and participated in training. Each subject received training in the three relations subject—verb—object, locatives, and possessives. At least one of these was a relation the subject had demonstrated in the observation sessions, and at least one was not.

In training, as many situations as possible were illustrated for each relation, the constraint being that the words involved, or equivalents of these words, must already be part of the subject's vocabulary. Teaching of vocabulary other than the experimenter's name was avoided. Any examples of the appropriate relations introduced by a subject were capitalized upon and used in training. The subject's spontaneous verbalizations in this way often determined the content of training for a particular session. Sample transcripts from the training sessions appear in appendix B.

Subject—verb—object training

In subject—verb—object training, most subjects were animate, and more or less familiar to the subject – himself, Mommy, the experimenter, and any other familiar people such as aunts, siblings, neighbors who might be present. Whenever possible, subject—verb—object relations were first illustrated using the subject, then his mother, then the experimenter. This arrangement, however, was extremely flexible. The objects were all familiar, and as often as possible, inanimate. Actions were clearly observable, familiar, and appropriate to the object involved. Some common situations were:

riding a bicycle	reading a book
throwing a ball	opening a door
shaking a rattle	opening or closing a box
breaking a balloon	blowing out a candle.

Because the results of the form-preference test, to be described in chapter 5, showed that the subject had few preferences for well-formed versus telegraphic, or child-formed sentences, both full sentences and two-word utterances were used as examples in the training sessions. Also, since preliminary observations indicated that some subjects holophrastically expressed the verb or action in the subject–verb–object relation, while some expressed the subject, both subject–verb and subject–object pairs were used as two-word examples. Whenever possible, the experimenter followed the subject's lead. If, for example, a subject said 'ball', the experimenter might say 'Lia ball'. If the subject said 'kick', the experimenter might say, 'Lia kicks'. At first, if Lia uttered the two-word relation, as rarely happened, she would be rewarded. The reward used was a clown face which lit up with Christmas tree lights. This did not seem to keep the subjects' attention, and scared one subject so the clown was abandoned and praise only used as a reward. It was hoped that the subject would first be praised for repeating a single word. Later he would be required to say two words, in any order. Still later, he must produce the two-word combination in the proper order only. Since, most subjects never produced two-word combinations, the experimenter continued to reward the subject for uttering one-half of the required relation. An intermediate procedure was also used, based on Kaye's (1968) discovery that a child who, for example, will not say 'open door' can often be induced to answer correctly the question 'open what?' The subject was praised for correctly answering, 'child what?' or 'Maris what?' Sometimes the question was asked in full form, e.g. 'Who kicked the ball?' and sometimes in shortened form, e.g. 'Who ball?'

Training for each subject was completely tape-recorded. In the case of all subjects except Lia, the first subject, an observer was present at all training and follow-up sessions. In addition to tape-recordings, the observer made notes of the contexts of all utterances; these notes were later incorporated into the transcripts. Two observers were employed. A male high school student served as the observer for Jessica and Katie; a female college student served as the observer for all other subjects.

Training for locatives

Two types of training were used for the locative relation. The first involved the manipulation of the single visible displacement which had been used during the sensory-motor testing. The second type involved a constant person who changed location. The training procedure was similar to that described for subject–verb–object training.

In the first type of training, involving displacement, the locative relation verbalized was the final location of the object which was moved. For example, the experimenter might place a marble in a cup as a subject watched. The experimenter would then say, 'Marble cup', giving the subject

or agent and the location, or the entire sentence, 'The marble is in the cup.'
Intermediate steps in training paralleled those described above. Some
examples which actually occurred are:

> marble cup (The marble is in the cup.)
> dolly pillow (The dolly is on the pillow.)
> baby bed (The baby is in the bed.)

The second type of training for the locative relation was used much
more often than the first. Three persons – the subject, the subject's mother,
and the experimenter – were used. For example, the experimenter might say
either 'Maris is in the chair' or 'Maris chair' as she was sitting in a chair
in the subject's view. The experimenter tried not to speak for several seconds, after she initially sat in the chair, so that the subject would not con-
fuse the action of sitting with the location 'chair'. Some common examples
were:

> Maris chair (Maris is in the chair.)
> Mommy rug (Mommy is on the rug.)
> [The subject] bed ([The subject] is on the bed)

Again, training was similar to that described for the subject–verb–object
relation.

Training for possessive relations

Although the experimenter tried at first to introduce only relations involving alienable possessions (McNeill, 1970b; Brown, 1973), things such as
objects of clothing which can be removed from their owner, the subject
often introduced relations involving an inalienable possession, such as a part
of the body. These examples were always followed through and trained.
The distinction between the two types of possessions is irrelevant to this
study. Again, steps in training were similar to those described above. Some
common situations were:

> Maris purse (It's Maris's purse.)
> Mommy coat (It's Mommy's coat.)
> clown eye (It's the clown's eye.)
> baby bottle (It's the baby's bottle.)
> [The subject] ball (It's [the subject's]ball)

The full form 'It's [name's] ——' was used because it is an appropriate answer to the question 'Whose —— is it?'

TESTING FOR RETENTION AND GENERALIZATION

Approximately four or five days after training was completed, the experimenter returned to the subject's home, accompanied by the observer. The original purpose of this visit was to determine whether acquisitions produced by training had become an integrated part of the subject's linguistic competence, i.e. whether they were stable and had generalized to new situations, as predicted in chapter 2. Since, in most cases, very little training had occurred, it was not appropriate to test for retention and generalization of two-word combinations; there were none to test. Nevertheless, the experimenter proceeded as closely as possible to the original plan. Except in two cases, Lia and Deanna, where the observer could not be present, the experimenter and the observer returned together for the follow-up session. The time lapse in days between the last training session and the follow-up session is shown in table 1 on page 34. In the case where a subject showed any evidence of successful training, the experimenter and the observer tested retention and generalization to as many new situations as possible. In cases in which no training had occurred, the experimenter and the observer continued training together. In the latter cases, this last session was in effect another training session, held after a short time lapse, with the biggest difference being that the observer participated actively in the training procedure for the only time.

FORM OF THE DATA AND DATA ANALYSIS

Because of the massive amount of data obtained during this study, it was not feasible to transcribe all the tape-recorded material. A sampling method was chosen in which about 20 per cent of the data, approximately four out of every twenty marker units of tape, was transcribed. Although this ratio was adhered to as closely as possible exceptions were made if, for example, a coherent segment lasted five or six units. The next segment would then be taken at a correspondingly greater distance. This sampling method was applied to all sessions for which an audible tape-recording was available. A total of six sessions, one each for Lia, Glynis, Katie, and Paula, and two for Felice, could not be transcribed because the tapes were ruined. Of these six, Lia's missing session and one of Felice's missing sessions were from the observation period, the remainder were training sessions. With the exception of seven sessions for Deanna, six for Andrew, one for Paula, and one for Felice, which were transcribed by the observer who had been present at these sessions, all transcription was done by the experimenter.

These tape-recorded samples provided the basic psycholinguistic data of the study. The classification system used for each utterance has been described earlier in this chapter. A thorough analysis of the data appears in chapter 4. The only material transcribed in addition to the samples was the proceedings of the sensory-motor and form-preference tests. These were transcribed verbatim for scoring purposes, but the transcripts were not included in the psycholinguistic data analysis, unless some of the material had also been transcribed in the regular sampling procedure.

4 The patterns of psycholinguistic and sensory-motor abilities

The results of this study are organized into four sections. First, results of the sensory-motor tests are presented, followed by results of the psycholinguistic data in the observation and training periods, then an analysis of changes in the psycholinguistic data from the observation period to the training and follow-up period, and finally, a comparison of the sensory-motor and psycholinguistic data during the observation period. This organization was chosen since it seemed to fit best the multiple goals of the study. One goal, of course, was an assessment of the general level of sensory-motor ability of these subjects, as well as a comparison of their abilities on specific cognitive and linguistic tasks which were proposed to be correlates. The observation period was used to obtain this information, as well as a description of the subject's psycholinguistic level at the time. Since the experimental portion of the study was a psycholinguistic training program, all changes in psycholinguistic performance from the observation to the training and follow-up period are crucial. A final comparison of sensory-motor and psycholinguistic abilities was reserved until the complete picture was available and it could therefore be considered in proper perspective.

RESULTS OF THE SENSORY-MOTOR TESTING

Six tests of sensory-motor ability were administered during the observation period. These included tests for two correlates of the subject–verb–object relation, one correlate of the locative relation, and tests to determine the subjects' level of ability in role playing, symbolic play, and deferred imitation. The results of these tests are presented in tables 2–7.

Correlate to the subject–verb–object relation:
using one object to act upon another

This task was administered to all ten subjects although as table 2 shows, four subjects refused to perform this task. Of the six subjects, who attempted

TABLE 2   *Sensory-motor tasks correlate to the subject–verb–object relation: actor-object task results*

S	Part 1 (Object A acts on object B)				Part 2 (Object B acts on object A)			
	Number trials[a]	Success	Failure	Refusal	Number trials[a]	Success	Failure	Refusal
Lia	1	0	0	1	0	0	0	0
Deanna	6	4	1	1	5	1	1	3
Glynis	5	1	0	4	1	1	0	0
Katie	2	0	0	2	many	0	0	many
Jordan	1	0	0	1	0	0	1	0
Jessica	5	1	4	0	3	2	0	1
Andrew	5	1	2	2	1	1	0	0
Ricky	1	0	0	1	0	0	0	0
Paula	1	1	0	0	1	1	0	0
Felice	2	1	0	1	1	1	0	0

[a] A trial continued until the subject lost interest. Trials usually included more than a single attempt by the experimenter to get the subject to perform the task.

the task, all were able to perform the required action correctly at least once, and all six were also able to reverse the task correctly at least once.

Correlate to the subject–verb–object relation:
the stacking-cups task

As table 3 shows, the results obtained on this task are roughly comparable to those obtained by Greenfield, Nelson, and Saltzman (1972), considering

TABLE 3   *Sensory-motor tasks correlate to the subject–verb–object relation: results of the stacking-cups task*

S[a]	Age	Type of structure				Per cent of each structure		
		Pairs	Pots	Sub-assemblies	Total	Pairs	Pots	Sub-assemblies
Katie	16(8)	5	5	1	11	45.5	45.5	9.0
Lia	16(24)	2	0	0	2	100	0	0
Glynis	16(26)	24	14	0	38	63.1	36.8	0
Jessica	17(6)	16	4	3	23	69.5	17.3	13.0
Andrew	17(17)	3	0	0	3	100	0	0
Felice	17(20)	3	2	1	6	50	33.3	16.7
Ricky	17(23)	2	0	0	2	100	0	0
Paula	18(17)	3	6	0	9	33.3	66.7	0
Deanna	19(11)	12	21	3	36	33.3	58.3	8.3
Jordan	22(13)	5	1	0	6	83.3	16.7	0

[a] Subjects are listed in order of increasing age on the date of testings. Ages are shown in months and days.

the methodological differences described in chapter 3. The simplest strategy, pairing, was dominant for seven subjects; the intermediate strategy, the 'pot strategy' was dominant for two of the older subjects; and the pairing and pot strategies were equally dominant for one subject. The most advanced, or 'sub-assembly' strategy was used by four of these young subjects, but was dominant for none. The dominant strategy appeared in 45.5 per cent to 100 per cent of the structures produced by each subject: eliminating the three cases in which three or fewer structures were produced, the dominant strategy represented 45.5 per cent to 83.3 per cent of a particular subject's structures.

Comparison of the two correlates to the subject–verb–object relation

Comparing subjects' performance on the stacking-cups task to the two-object task, it is clear that there is more consistency among subjects who showed the least advanced strategies on the stacking-cups task than among those who were most advanced. Of the three subjects who produced only pairs, and would engage only in three or fewer trials in stacking cups, two, Lia, and Ricky also refused to attempt the two-object task. The third member of this group, Andrew, demonstrated an inconsistent pattern of success, failure, and refusal on the two-object task. The next subject developmentally on the stacking-cups task, Jordan, also had no success on the two-object task. Considering the four subjects who created sub-assemblies on the stacking-cups task, Katie, Jessica, Felice, and Deanna, only Felice also had at least one success on both parts of the two-object task, Jessica and Deanna had at least one success on either part A or part B, and Katie had refused to co-operate.

The correlate to the locative relation: displacement

As described above, the cognitive correlate to the locative relation was assumed to be the ability to find an object which had been hidden. The task was administered to all ten subjects, but no data is available for two subjects who refused to attempt the task. In one case, Glynis, the task was administered out of the usual experimental sequence, two weeks after the follow-up session.

As table 4 shows, all eight subjects who co-operated on this task successfully performed a single visible displacement at least once. One subject who refused to co-operate, Lia, provided spontaneous evidence that she was

TABLE 4   *Sensory-motor tasks correlate to the locative relation: results of the displacement task*

S	Age	Visible displacements				Invisible displacements			
		one		two		one		two	
		Successes	Total trials	Successes	Total trials	Successes	Total trials	Successes	Total trials
Lia[a]									
Deanna	20(6)	2	5	0	4	0	2	0	1
Glynis[b]	17(26)	3	4	2	7	3	4	2	11
Katie	16(17)	4	7	0	2	0	2	0	0
Jordan	21(19)	2	3	3	5	0	2	0	0
Jessica	16(29)	1	3	2	3	0	0	0	0
Andrew[a]									
Ricky	17(23)	1	6	1	1	0	2	0	0
Paula	18(21)	1	2	1	3	2	4	0	0
Felice	17(23)	1	many	0	0	0	0	0	0

[a] Task not administered.
[b] Glynis was tested two weeks after the follow-up session. All other subjects were tested during the observation period.

able to retrieve objects such as beads which had rolled behind sofas and chairs while she was watching. Five of the eight subjects tested were able to retrieve an object after two visible displacements. Two were able to retrieve after a single invisible displacement, and one, Glynis, after two invisible displacements. Glynis was tested two weeks after the close of the study. In no case did any subject who was unable to perform the task at any level of testing perform successfully at a higher level, e.g. no subject successfully performed invisible displacements who had not succeeded at two visible displacements.

Test of symbolic play

As explained in chapter 3, this test was included as one measure of the subjects' general level of representational ability. The subjects' co-operation on this task was generally poor. In order to supplement the task, all spontaneous instances in which a subject represented with gestures something which was not currently happening were recorded and are included along with data from the formal test in table 5. Eight subjects demonstrated this ability at least once, and of these eight, six illustrated at least two different activities symbolically. Only one subject who provided experimental examples did not also provide spontaneous examples. Of the two subjects who demonstrated no symbolic ability during the experimental period,

TABLE 5   *Sensory-motor tasks: examples of symbolic play*

S	Trials – including spontaneous examples	Successes (Total)	Spontaneous examples	Failures	Refusals	Number of different successes[a]
Lia	many (7 planned)[b]	many + 5[b]	many	1	1	2
Deanna	4	0	0	0	4	0
Glynis	13	4	2	0	9	2
Katie	7	0	0	1	6	0
Jordan	15	14	7	1	0	5
Jessica	5	2	0	0	3	2
Andrew	9	2	2	2	5	1
Ricky	13	10	7	0	3	4
Paula	9	2	2	3	4	1
Felice	9	7	5	2	0	2

[a] This column shows the number of different actions depicted in symbolic play.

[b] Spontaneous examples are listed as 'many'. The number shown refers to formal trials.

Andrew's mother, at least, insisted that he provided many examples when the experimenter was not present.

Test of role playing ability

Table 6 indicates that little was learned about the subjects' role playing ability during this study. Only one subject attempted the task. In all cases, it was the experimenter's subjective impression that the subject did not understand the instructions, but no variation and no amount of coaxing improved the situation. In addition, none of the ten subjects provided any spontaneous examples of role playing ability during the course of the experiment, and none of the subjects' mothers could recall any examples.

TABLE 6   *Sensory-motor tasks: role playing task*

S	Trials	Successes	Failures	Refusals to try	Spontaneous examples of role playing
Lia	2	0	0	2	0
Deanna	3	0	0	3	0
Glynis	3	0	0	3	0
Katie	0	0	0	0	0
Jordan	0	0	0	0	0
Jessica	5	1	0	4	0
Andrew	3	0	0	3	0
Ricky	3	0	0	3	0
Paula	0	0	0	0	0
Felice	6	0	3	3	0

TABLE 7   *Sensory-motor tasks: imitation task results*

S	Immediate imitation		Deferred imitation		Spontaneous deferred imitation
	Trials	Successes	Trials	Successes	Number of examples
Lia	5	0	3	3	6
Deanna	2	2	2	0	1
Glynis	2	0	2	2	0
Katie	many	0	many	0	0
Jordan	5	3	0	0	many
Jessica	2	0	1	1	0
Andrew	5	4	2	0	2
Ricky	1	0	0	0	0
Paula	8	2	many	0	many
Felice	3	2	0	2	4

This lack of spontaneous examples was in contrast to all other sensory-motor abilities examined in this study.

Test of imitation and deferred imitation

Again, it was difficult to obtain the subjects' co-operation, and again, a 'trial' as listed on table 7 represented several attempts to get a subject to perform the task. The task was administered to all ten subjects. In addition, table 7 includes all spontaneous examples of deferred imitation which occurred in the experimenter's presence.

Five subjects complied with the experimenter's request to imitate the action immediately after its demonstration. Eight subjects provided examples of deferred imitation; of these, four provided only spontaneous examples, e.g. holding a hand up to an ear and pretending to talk into a telephone receiver. It is of particular interest that three of these eight subjects, Lia, Glynis, and Andrew, produced deferred imitations of items which they had not imitated immediately after presentation. Of the two subjects who displayed no deferred imitations, there was no reason to assume that they had demonstrated this activity before. On the other hand, the subjects who displayed this ability during the study displayed it at other times as well, according to their mothers' reports.

RESULTS OF THE TEST FOR FORM-PREFERENCE

The results of the test for form-preference in the obeying of commands are presented in table 8. It is immediately obvious that the number of com-

TABLE 8 *Results of the test for form-preference commands to which subjects respond*[a]

S	No. of commands given	No. of commands to which subject responds	Pairs to which subject responds	Child forms	All full forms	Full forms with no indirect object	Ratio of child to all full forms	Ratio of child forms plus forms with no indirect object to full forms which include indirect objects
Lia	20	8	1	4	4	4	4:4	8:0
Deanna	19	6	1	3	3	1	3:3	4:2
Glynis	18	7	1	3	4	2	3:4	5:2
Katie	19	3	0	1	2	1	1:2	2:1
Jordan	20	9	2	3	5	1	3:6	4:5
Jessica	20	8	0	4	4	1	4:4	5:3
Andrew	20	9	1	5	4	2	5:4	7:2
Ricky	20	9	2	5	4	3	5:4	8:1
Paula	19	6	2	3	3	3	3:3	6:0
Felice	19	6	0	2	4	2	2:4	4:2

[a] Pairs are child and full forms which express the same command, e.g. 'Throw ball' (child) and 'Throw me the ball' (full). This is *one* pair. 'Child forms' are two-word commands, e.g. 'Ring bell'. 'Full forms' are commands given in complete, correct English. This includes forms with indirect objects, e.g. 'Pull me the wheelbarrow', and without indirect objects, e.g. 'Break the cup'.

mands obeyed by any subject is far fewer than the total number of commands administered. If one considers the ratio of all child-form to all complete or adult-form commands, only two subjects, Jordan and Felice, display any clear preference in the type of commands obeyed; both obeyed twice as many adult as child-form commands.

If one groups commands which are well-formed, but contain no indirect object, e.g. 'Squeeze the pillow', together with the child-form commands and compares these to adult forms which contain indirect objects, such as 'Push me the wheelbarrow', the pattern changes radically. Now only Jordan prefers the longer commands and all other subjects markedly prefer the shorter forms. Based on the number of commands included in the task, however, one would expect the ratio of no preference to be a 3 : 1 response in favor of short commands. In fact, only five subjects showed a higher ratio, so again there was no difference in preference based upon the number of words in the command. These results can be compared to those obtained by Nelson (1973). At thirteen to seventeen months of age, her subjects preferred longer sentences, in a range from one to five words, but at age seventeen to twenty months, comparable to the age of the subjects in this study, there was no preference in the obeying of commands two, four, and six words long.

THE PSYCHOLINGUISTIC PICTURE FOR THE OBSERVATION PERIOD

The psycholinguistic data for the observation period consist of two major parts: the pattern of holophrastic and non-holophrastic single-word utterances, and the pattern of sequences of holophrastic utterances and two-word combinations.

The pattern of holophrastic and non-holophrastic single-word utterances

The classification of single-word utterances is presented in table 9. Looking first at the total proportion of the subject's single-word speech which could be classified as holophrastic according to the criteria described in chapters 2 and 3, one notes that this ranges from 29 per cent to 69 per cent. All ten subjects produced substantial numbers of holophrases, and in eight of the ten cases, 40 per cent or more of the subjects' single-word utterances were classifiable as holophrastic. The two subjects who produced the smallest proportion of holophrastic speech also produced large numbers of non-classifiable non-holophrastic utterances.

TABLE 9 *Holophrastic and non-holophrastic single-word utterances during the observation period expressed as percentages of each subject's single-word speech).*

| S | No. utt. | Holophrastic | | | | | | | | | | Non-holophrastic | | | |
		S–V–O	Loc.	Pos.	Want	Neg.	Where	Attrib.	Salutes	Other	Total[a] holophrases	Name	Rep.	Other	Total[a] non-holophrastic speech
Lia	179	21	7	0[b]	13	0.55	0	4	4	11	56	23	6	17	46
Deanna	283	34	0	0	25	3	1	4	0	2	69	20	3	9	31
Glynis	198	4	0	3	29	6	2	0	8	12	64	3	2	31	36
Katie	157	4	0	0	11	6	0	1	0.63	6	29	34	6	31	70
Jordan	177	9	0	0	7	2	0	0	5	6	29	27	24	21	72
Jessica	184	23	0	0	14	1	1	0	0	4	44	22	20	14	56
Andrew	179	9	0	0	22	2	1	0	0	17	49	30	8	12	50
Ricky	224	16	0.55	0.44	14	8	3	0	6	8	54	4	8	37	48
Paula	328	8	0.3	0	25	0.60	2	1	0	2	40	35	19	7	61
Felice	101	12	1	0	24	0	0	0	3	4	45	32	19	5	56
All subjects	2010	13	0.9	0.3	18	2.9	1	1	3	7	48	23	12	19	53

S–V–O = subject–verb–object.

Loc. = locative.

Pos. = possessive.

Want = 'I want' = holophrases of type 'I want a ——' or 'I want to ——', in which missing word is expressed.

Neg. = negative.

Where = holophrases of type, '*where* is the ——?' or '*where* did the —— go?'; where is expressed.

Attrib. = attribute.

Salutes = 'hi', 'bye', 'hello', and 'bye-bye'.

Other = other relational uses of single words as described in chapters 2 and 3.

Total holophrases = sum of previous nine columns.

Name = simple naming.

Rep. = repetitions of words adult has just expressed.

Other = undefined or unclassifiable use of single words.

Total non-holophrastic speech = sum of naming, repetitions, and other non-holophrastic usages.

[a] In this and all following tables, totals do not always add to 100 due to rounding.

[b] Although examples did not appear in the sampling, Lia did provide holophrastic examples of possessives.

TABLE 10   *Subject–verb–object holophrases during the observation period: percentage of subjects, verbs, and objects expressed (in percentages of each subject's single-word speech)*

S	Number utterances	% Subjects	% Verbs	% Objects	Total %
Lia	179	19	2	0	21
Deanna	283	14	17	3	34
Glynis	198	4	0	0	4
Katie	157	0	2	2	4
Jordan	177	5	4	0	9
Jessica	184	3	21	0	23
Andrew	179	4	5	0	9
Ricky	224	15	0.89	0	16
Paula	328	8	0	0.30	8
Felice	102	9	3	0	12
All Subjects	2010	8.1	5.4	0.53	13.0

Considering the ten subjects as a group, the largest category of holophrastic utterances was the 'I want' group as in 'I want the *doll*' and 'I want to *read* the book'; the italicized word was the word actually uttered by the subject. There was also a large proportion of subject–verb–object holophrases, and for some subjects this category exceeded the 'I want' category. Table 10 gives a breakdown of the subject–verb–object category, indicating which element of the relation was actually expressed in the holophrase. The most common category expressed was subjects, e.g. 'dai' (= train) as in 'The *train* stops.' Two subjects, Deanna and Jessica, expressed more verbs than subjects, e.g. 'read' as in 'Mommy *read*(s) the book.' Very few objects, e.g. 'noise' as in 'The tape recorder makes *noise*' were expressed by these subjects during the observation period. As mentioned in chapter 3, it can be difficult to decide whether an uttered noun should be glossed as subject or object. The object category was used only when this choice seemed obvious, as in the example above. All subjects who used a large number of 'subject holophrases' also did quite a lot of non-holophrastic naming of objects. On the other hand, five subjects, Katie, Jordan, Andrew, Paula, and Felice, all did much naming but did not use large numbers of subject holophrases.

Considering only the three target relations for this study: subject–verb–object, locatives, and possessives, table 9 indicates that only the subject–verb–object relation was expressed by all ten subjects. Four subjects expressed the locative relation; two other subjects expressed the possessive relation. All ten subjects thus met the criterion for continuation in the study of using at least one, but not all three of the target relations. There was some difficulty in choosing the subjects in this manner. Due to the nature of the sampling procedure, explained in chapter 3, upon which all the tables are based, Lia does not appear to be expressing the possessive relation. During one session, however, Lia did provide clear evidence that she was using this relation; the segment did not appear in the sample and thus is not reflected in table 9. Lia was included in the study, because at that time she was not believed to be expressing the locative relation. With all the data available, it now appears that Lia was actually using all three relations at the time. This did not occur in the case of the other nine subjects.

It is obvious from table 9 that the three target holophrases were not the three holophrastic relations which a subject expressed most often. 'Where-holophrases', negatives, attributives, and salutes were all used as many and more times than the locative and possessive relations by individual subjects. The three target holophrases were chosen for the reasons given in chapter 2, not because they were most frequent.

Table 9 also reveals that non-holophrastic utterances comprise a major portion of the subjects' speech at this time; in four cases non-holophrastic utterances comprise 55 per cent or more of the subjects' single-word speech. The three categories of non-holophrastic speech: naming, repetitions, and other utterances have all been defined in chapter 3. The only point which needs repetition here is the difference between holophrastic expression of a subject and non-holophrastic naming. Again, the subject category was used when an object had been present and the focus of the subject's attention, but the subject did not utter the word until some action occurred involving the object, e.g. a doll falling off a chair, or a train stopping in front of him. Simple naming was self-explanatory; a subject uttered the name of an object which was not involved in any action. This category of simple naming represented 20 per cent or more of the subjects' single-word speech in eight cases. In seven cases, the percentage of naming and the percentage of subject usage was discrepant by 12 per cent or more; this supports the claim that the distinction between naming and subject usage is valid.

During the observation period, the percentage of single-word utterances classifiable as simple repetitions of the immediately preceding adult utterance ranged from 2 per cent to 24 per cent of single-word speech. The subject producing the highest proportion of repetitions, Jordan, also tied in producing the lowest proportion of total holophrastic speech, and the two subjects with the lowest proportions of simple repetitions, Glynis and Deanna, also produced the highest proportions of total holophrastic speech.

Seven subjects produced 12 per cent or more of their single-word utter-

ances which were classified as non-holophrastic 'other' utterances which had
no recognizable linguistic or extralinguistic antecedent, and which did not
fit this classification system. There was no consistent relation across the
ten subjects between the amount of this unclassifiable speech, and total
proportion of holophrastic compared to non-holophrastic utterances.

*Sequences of holophrases and two-word combinations during
the observation period*

Tables 11 and 12 indicate the sequences of holophrastic utterances and
the two-word combinations which appeared during the observation period;
the basis for classification into relational and non-relational groupings is
presented in chapter 3. In all cases, the number of both sequences and
combinations is small. Felice did produce a somewhat higher proportion,
approximately 14 per cent of relational combinations, although this included no examples of the three target relations. Almost none of the
sequences of holophrases, and none of the combinations appeared in inverted word-order, e.g. there were few instances of 'purse Mommy' instead
of 'Mommy purse' for 'Mommy's purse'. All ten subjects produced some
sequences, and eight produced some combinations during the observation
period.

Tables 13 and 14 present data which bear on the issue of utterance
length and the emergence of two-'word' combinatorial utterances, the percentage of meaningful single-word utterances which were preceded or
followed by non-meaningful sounds. The tables show that all subjects made
some combinations of sounds with meaningful words, and that in a small
portion of these utterances the non-meaningful sound followed rather
than preceded the recognizable word. Combinations with 'mm' were less
common than combinations with the schwa sound, which in turn were
less common than total combinations with all other sounds. Possible theoretical implications of these findings will be discussed in chapter 5.

*Other data on awareness of linguistic relations: responses to
questions, and separated sequences*

Table 15 presents other data intended to clarify the main issues. As described in chapter 3, the subjects' response to adult questions, and widely
separated sequences were both tallied in the hope that such data would
provide additional insight into the subjects' awareness of linguistic relations.

TABLE 11   *Sequences of holophrases, and two-word combinations during the observation period (in percentages of each subject's single-word plus combinatorial speech)*ᵃ

S	No. utt.	Sequences						Combinations					
		Relational			Other	Total	Non-rel.	Relational			Other	Total	Non-rel.
		S–V–O	Loc.	Pos.				S–V–O	Loc.	Pos.			
Lia	179	1.11	0.55	0	0.55	2.23	0.55	0	0	0	0	0	0
Deanna	283	0.70	0	0	0	0.70	0.35	0	0	0	0	0	0
Glynis	202	0.50	0	0.99	2.48	3.96	0	0.50	0	0.50	0.99	1.98	0
Katie	160	0	0	0	0.63	0.63	0	0	0	0	0.56	0.56	0
Jordan	179	0	0	0	0	0	1.12	0.56	0	0	0.56	1.12	0
Jessica	188	0	0	0	0.53	0.53	0	0.53	0	0	1.06	1.60	0.53
Andrew	182	0	0	0	0.55	0.55	0	0	0	0	1.65	1.65	0
Ricky	241	0.41	0	0	2.08	2.50	1.24	0.83	0	0	2.90	3.73	3.32
Paula	330	0	0	0	0.60	0.60	0.91	0	0	0	0.60	0.60	0
Felice	118	0	0	0	0.85	0.85	0	0	0	0	13.56	13.56	0.85
All subjects	2062	0.29	0.05	0.10	0.82	1.26	0.48	0.24	0	0.05	1.65	1.94	0.53

ᵃ This table includes all sequences of holophrases and all two-word combinations, including those which occur in 'inverted' order, e.g. 'ball kick' instead of 'kick ball'.

TABLE 12 *Inverted sequences of holophrases and two-word combinations during the observation period (in percentages of each subject's single-word plus combinatorial speech)*[a]

S	No. utt.	Sequences						Combinations					
		Relational				Total	Non-rel.	Relational				Total	Non-rel.
		S–V–O	Loc.	Pos.	Other			S–V–O	Loc.	Pos.	Other		
Lia	179	0	0	0	0	0	0	0	0	0	0	0	0
Deanna	283	0	0	0	0	0	0	0	0	0	0	0	0
Glynis	202	0.50	0	0	0.50	0.99	0	0	0	0	0	0	0
Katie	160	0	0	0	0	0	0	0	0	0	0	0	0
Jordan	179	0	0	0	0	0	0	0	0	0	0	0	0
Jessica	188	0	0	0	0	0	0	0	0	0	0	0	0
Andrew	182	0	0	0	0	0	0	0	0	0	0	0	0
Ricky	241	0	0	0	0	0	0	0	0	0	0	0	0
Paula	330	0	0	0	0.30	0.30	0	0	0	0	0	0	0
Felice	118	0	0	0	0	0	0	0	0	0	0	0	0
All subjects	2062	0.05	0	0	0.10	0.15	0	0	0	0	0	0	0

[a] See table 11.

TABLE 13 *Combinations of meaningful words with non-meaningful sounds during the observation period (in percentages of each subject's single-word plus combinatorial speech)* [a]

S	Total utt.	'mm' + word	'uh' + word	other sounds + word
Lia	179	4	3	9
Deanna	283	2	5	3
Glynis	202	0	7	12
Katie	160	4	6	11
Jordan	179	1	17	16
Jessica	188	2	3	17
Andrew	182	3	9	9
Ricky	241	6	12	18
Paula	330	0.90	6	4
Felice	118	0	2	0
All subjects	2062	2.3	7.0	9.8

[a] This table includes 'inverted' combinations in which the non-meaningful sound follows rather than precedes the meaningful word.

A small number of correct responses to questions were provided by eight subjects. Only relationally appropriate answers to questions are included here. Only two subjects produced holophrastic utterances which might be interpreted as widely separated sequences.

TABLE 14 *Percentages of combinations of meaningful words with non-meaningful sounds during the observation period which appeared in inverted order (in percentages of each subject's single-word plus combinatorial speech)* [a]

S	Total utt.	word + 'mm'	word + 'uh'	word + other sounds
Lia	179	0	0	0
Deanna	283	0	0	0.35
Glynis	202	0	0	0.49
Katie	160	0.63	1	2
Jordan	179	0	0.56	2
Jessica	188	0	0.53	4
Andrew	182	0	0.54	1
Ricky	241	0	2	1
Paula	330	0	0.60	1
Felice	118	0	0.84	0
All subjects	2062	0.05	0.58	1.26

[a] See table 13.

TABLE 15   *Percentage of correct responses to questions, and widely separated sequences of holophrases during the observation period (in percentages of each subject's single-word speech)[a]*

S	No. utt.	Responses to questions	Widely separated sequences[b]
Lia	179	0.55	0.55
Deanna	283	1	2
Glynis	198	4	0
Katie	157	0	0
Jordan	177	3	0
Jessica	184	2	0
Andrew	179	1	0
Ricky	224	2	0
Paula	328	0	0
Felice	102	3	0
All subjects	2010	1.7	0.3

[a] Correct answers to questions = child's answer to adult's question, when child's response indicates that he understands the relation involved, e.g. 'Whose purse is it?' 'Mommy'.
[b] Widely separated sequences of holophrases = two holophrases uttered by a child which might exemplify a relation if they had occurred without a pause, e.g. 'Daddy' (long pause) 'home'.

Summary of the psycholinguistic pattern during the observation period

Based on the data presented in tables 9–15, all ten subjects are classified as operating in the single-word period of language acquisition. Some have begun to produce a few two-word combinations, but none with any frequency or regularity. Most subjects show signs that they are nearing the end of this holophrastic period. Nine of the ten have begun to produce sequences of holophrases which would have been considered to be grammatical combinations had they been uttered more closely together. Of the sequences and combinations which appear, few are in inverted word order. Eight of ten subjects also demonstrate their understanding of relational concepts by their ability to appropriately answer questions.

All ten subjects can be classified as holophrastic in their single-word usage to a substantial degree. Eight subjects use 40 per cent or more of their single-word speech holophrastically. The pattern of holophrastic usage varies considerably from subject to subject.

THE PSYCHOLINGUISTIC PICTURE DURING THE TRAINING PERIOD

The same types of data were collected during the training period as during observation. This includes the pattern of holophrastic and non-holophrastic utterances in single-word speech, the pattern of sequences of holophrases and two-word combinations, and other information pertinent to the subjects' understanding of linguistic relations. In addition, data describing the nature of the training procedure, particularly as it differed from the observation period, will be discussed. These data consist of the number and types of examples of linguistic relations provided to the child by adults.

The pattern of holophrastic and non-holophrastic utterances

The pattern of holophrastic and non-holophrastic utterances for sessions in which intervention occurred, i.e. training and follow-up sessions, is shown in table 16. In only one case was less than 40 per cent of the subjects' single-word speech used holophrastically; the range for holophrastic expression in single-word speech is now 32 per cent to 63 per cent, with a mean of 51 per cent for all the subjects considered together. The most common relation used holophrastically is the 'I want' relation. Considering the three target relations for this study, the subject–verb–object relation is expressed much more frequently than locative and possessive. Table 17 shows the expression of the three components of the subject–verb–object relation. Subjects are expressed most frequently, a very few objects are expressed, but now a substantial number of verbs are also being expressed holophrastically. Five subjects are now using the locative relation holophrastically, and eight of ten subjects use holophrastic possessives.

Non-holophrastic naming and repetition or imitation of an adult's preceding utterance also account for substantial proportions of the subjects' speech during the intervention period. The range for naming is from 9 to 26 per cent of single-word speech. The range for repetition is from 11 to 47 per cent of single-word speech. Paula, the subject with by far the highest proportion of repetition or imitation, also had the lowest total proportion of holophrastic speech. For the other subjects, however, there is no clear relationship between proportion of repetition and proportion of holophrastic speech. It is extremely interesting that during the observation period another subject, Jordan, also showed both the highest proportion of repetition, and the lowest proportion of holophrastic speech. During training, Jordan is the only subject who is now repeating proportionally less often (4 per cent less) than during observation; his proportion of holophrastic speech, however, has increased tremendously from 29 per cent during training to 55 per cent during observation. In contrast, Paula has

TABLE 16 *Holophrastic and non-holophrastic single-word utterances during the training and follow-up period (expressed as percentages of each subject's single-word speech).*

S	No. utt.	S–V–O	Loc.	Pos.	Want	Neg.	Where	Attrib.	Salutes	Other	Total[a] holophrases	Name	Rep.	Other	Total[a] non-holophrastic speech
											(Holophrastic)				(Non-holophrastic)
Lia	542	6	6	5	15	0.18	4	0	0	10	46	22	21	7	50
Deanna	547	22	0	0	31	0.09	0.54	3	0	4	62	13	11	13	37
Glynis	322	8	2	1	19	8	0	0.31	7	16	61	10	16	13	39
Katie	109	17	0	0	14	11	0.91	0	2	0.91	45	25	12	18	55
Jordan	235	10	2	0.85	10	4	0.85	0.42	14	13	55	12	20	13	45
Jessica	338	5	2	1	13	9	0	7	5	13	54	12	20	14	46
Andrew	204	14	0	0.49	21	3	2	8	1	14	63	10	17	11	37
Ricky	383	4	0	1	5	25	0.26	0.26	4	9	49	9	11	31	51
Paula	331	3	0.60	5	17	2	2	0.86	0	0.30	32	16	47	6	69
Felice	232	28	0	1	5	1	0	3	0.43	3	41	26	23	10	59
All subjects	3232	12	1.3	2	15	6.3	1.1	2.2	3.3	8.4	51	16	20	14	49

S–V–O = subject–verb–object.
Loc. = locative.
Pos. = possessive.
Want = 'I want' = holophrases of type 'I want a ——', or 'I want to ——' in which missing word is word expressed.
Neg. = negative.
Where = holophrases of the type '*Where* is the ——?' or '*Where* did the —— go?'; where is expressed.
Attrib. = attributive.
Salutes = 'hi', 'bye', 'hello', and 'bye-bye'.
Other holophrases = other relational uses of single words as described in Chapters 2 and 3.
Total holophrases = sum of first nine columns.
Name = simple naming.
Rep. = repetitions of words adult has just expressed.
Other = undefined or unclassifiable use of single words.
Total non-holophrastic speech = sum of naming, repetition, and other non-holophrastic usages.
[a] Totals may not 100 due to rounding.

TABLE 17　*Subject–verb–object holophrases during the training and follow-up period: percentage of subjects, verbs, and objects expressed (in percentages of each subject's single-word speech).*

S	No. utt.	% Subjects	% Verbs	% Objects	% Total
Lia	542	6	0	0	6
Deanna	547	8	12	2	22
Glynis	333	8	0	0	8
Katie	109	8	8	0	17
Jordan	235	9	0.85	0	10
Jessica	338	3	1	0.88	5
Andrew	194	7	7	0	14
Ricky	381	4	0.52	0	4
Paula	331	3	0.60	0	3
Felice	233	6	18	4	28
All subjects	3232	6.3	4.6	0.7	11.7

markedly increased repetition from 19 per cent during observation to 47 per cent during training, while decreasing holophrastic expression from 40 to 32 per cent.

The pattern of sequences of holophrases and two-word combinations

Tables 18 and 19 present findings for the combination of non-meaningful sounds with meaningful words, parallel to tables 13 and 14 for the observation period. Again, all subjects make small numbers of combinations of recognizable words with mm, schwa, and other sounds, in increasing order

TABLE 18　*Percentage of combinations of meaningful words with non-meaningful sounds during the training and follow-up period (in percentages of each subject's single-word plus combinatorial speech)* [a]

S	No. utt.	'mm' + word	'uh' + word	Other sounds + word
Lia	553	10	3	5
Deanna	548	0	2	4
Glynis	333	1	8	8
Katie	115	3	8	14
Jordan	248	4	10	11
Jessica	361	2	3	7
Andrew	213	0.47	1	5
Ricky	404	2	9	14
Paula	336	0.29	4	2
Felice	261	0	4	4
All subjects	3372	2.3	5.2	7.4

[a] 'Inverted examples', in which the sound followed rather than preceded the word, are included in the totals given here.

TABLE 19 *Percentage of combinations of meaningful words with non-meaningful sounds which appeared in inverted order during training and follow-up period (in percentages of each subject's single-word plus combinatorial speech)*

S	No. utt.	Word + 'mm'	Word + 'uh'	Word + other sounds
Lia	553	0	0	0
Deanna	548	0	0	0
Glynis	333	0	0.30	3
Katie	115	0	0.86	0.86
Jordan	248	0	2	4
Jessica	361	0	0.27	0.27
Andrew	213	0	0.47	0.94
Ricky	404	0	1	2
Paula	336	0	0.89	0.29
Felice	261	0	2	2
All subjects	3372	0	0.6	1.3

of frequency. Again, too, in all but a very few cases, the sound precedes rather than follows the meaningful word.

The proportion of sequences of holophrases and of two-word combinations during the training and follow-up sessions is shown in tables 20–23. Six of the ten subjects produced sequences involving one or more of the three target relations; all ten subjects produced sequences expressing some kind of linguistic relation. Nine of the ten subjects expressed some relations in combinatorial form; all nine of these subjects expressed at least one of the three target relations in combination. The proportion of the subjects' total speech represented by relational sequences and combinations was small for all subjects. There were also some non-relational sequences and combinations, but in both cases, a Wilcoxon signed-ranks matched-pairs test showed these to be significantly fewer than their relational counterparts. Table 21 indicates that almost no combinations and not quite half the sequences appeared in inverted order. The theoretical significance of this finding will be discussed in chapter 5.

Comparing the expression of sequences and combinations for the three target relations which, of course, was specifically encouraged by the training procedure, to the expression of other relations, the training does not seem to have specifically influenced the expression of sequences. Only three subjects produced more target sequences than non-target, and another two subjects produced equal amounts of target and non-target sequences. For combinatorial expression, however, the situation is very different. One subject produced no combinations of any kind. Of the remaining nine

TABLE 20 *Sequences of holophrases, and two-word combinations during the training period^a (expressed in percentages of each subject's single-word plus combinatorial speech)*

S	No. utt.	Sequences						Combinations					
		S–V–O	Relational			Total	Non-rel.	S–V–O	Relational			Total	Non-rel.
			Loc.	Pos.	Other				Loc.	Pos.	Other		
Lia	477	0	0	0.20	0.41	0.62	0.83	0.20	0.62	0	0.20	1.04	0
Deanna	502	0.79	0	0.19	0.59	1.59	0.99	0.19	0	0	0	0.19	0
Glynis	293	0	1.02	0	1.02	2.04	1.02	0	0.34	0.68	0.68	1.70	1.70
Katie	105	1.90	0	0	0	1.90	0	4.76	0	0	0	4.76	0
Jordan	214	0	0.93	0	0.93	1.86	1.86	2.33	0.46	0.93	0.93	4.67	0
Jessica	299	0	0	0	1.67	1.67	1.00	2.00	0.83	0.66	2.67	5.68	0.33
Andrew	176	0	0	0	0.56	0.56	0	0	0	0.56	2.84	3.40	1.13
Ricky	348	0	0	0	3.44	3.44	2.29	1.14	0	0.28	2.58	4.02	2.29
Paula	242	0	0	0	0.41	0.41	0.82	0	0	0	0	0	0
Felice	216	1.85	0	0	0	1.85	0	6.19	0	0	2.77	9.72	0
All subjects	2872	0.45	0.20	0.04	0.90	1.60[b]	0.88[b]	1.68	0.23	0.33	1.27	3.52[c]	0.55[c]

^a Sequences and combinations produced during the follow-up session are presented in a separate table.
^b $p < 0.05$, two-tailed, $n = 9$, Wilcoxon signed-ranks, matched-pairs test.
^c $p < 0.01$, two-tailed, $n = 8$, Wilcoxon signed-ranks, matched-pairs test.

TABLE 21 *Inverted sequences of holophrases and two-word combinations during the training period (expressed in percentages of each subjects' single-word plus combinatorial speech)*

| | | Sequences | | | | | | Combinations | | | | | |
| | | Relational | | | | | Non-rel. | Relational | | | | | Non-rel. |
S	No. Utt.	S–V–O	Loc.	Pos.	Other	Total		S–V–O	Loc.	Pos.	Other	Total	
Lia	477	0	0	0.20	0	0.20	0	0	0	0	0	0	0
Deanna	502	0.59	0	0	0.39	0.99	0	0	0	0	0	0	0
Glynis	293	0	0	0	0.35	0.35	0	0	0	0	0	0	0
Katie	105	0.95	0	0	0	0.95	0	0	0	0	0	0	0
Jordan	214	0	0	0	0	0	0	0	0	0	0	0	0
Jessica	299	0	0	0	0	0	0	0	0.46	0	0	0.46	0
Andrew	176	0	0	0	0	0	0	0	0	0	0	0	0
Ricky	348	0	0	0	1.43	1.43	0	0	0	0	0	0	0
Paula	242	0	0	0	0	0	0	0	0	0	0	0	0
Felice	216	0.46	0	0	0	0.46	0	0	0	0	0	0	0
All subjects	2872	0.20	0	0.02	0.22	0.39	0	0	0.05	0	0	0.05	0

TABLE 22 *Sequences of holophrases and two-word combinations during the follow-up session expressed in percentages of each subject's single-word plus combinatorial speech)[a]*

| S | No. utt. | Sequences | | | | | | Combinations | | | | | |
| | | | Relational | | | | Non-rel. | | Relational | | | | Non-rel. |
		S–V–O	Loc.	Pos.	Other	Total		S–V–O	Loc.	Pos.	Other	Total	
Lia	76	0	1.31	5.26	0	6.57	0	0	1.31	0	0	1.31	0
Deanna	46	0	2.17	0	0	2.17	0	0	0	0	0	0	0
Glynis	40	0	0	0	0	0	0	0	0	0	0	0	0
Katie	10	0	0	0	0	0	0	0	20.0	0	0	20.0	0
Jordan	34	0	0	0	0	0	0	0	0	0	0	0	0
Jessica	62	0	0	0	1.61	1.61	0	0	3.22	0	8.06	11.29	0
Andrew	37	0	0	0	0	0	0	2.70	0	0	0	2.70	0
Ricky	56	0	0	0	0	0	7.14	0	0	0	8.92	8.92	0
Paula	94	0	0	1.06	0	1.06	0	5.31	0	0	0	5.31	0
Felice	45	0	0	0	0	0	0	6.66	2.22	4.44	0	13.33	0
All subjects	500	0	0.35	0.63	0.16	1.14	0.71	1.45	2.68	0.44	1.70	6.29	0

[a] This table includes all sequences of holophrases and two-word combinations, including those occurring in 'inverted' word order.

TABLE 23 *Inverted sequences of holophrases and two-word combinations during the follow-up session (expressed in percentages of each subject's single-word plus combinatorial speech)*

| | | Sequences | | | | | | Combinations | | | | | |
| | | | Relational | | | | | | Relational | | | | |
S	No. utt.	S–V–O	Loc.	Pos.	Other	Total	Non-rel.	S–V–O	Loc.	Pos.	Other	Total	Non-rel.
Lia	76	0	1.31	3.94	0	5.26	0	0	1.31	0	0	1.31	0
Deanna	46	0	0	0	0	0	0	0	0	0	0	0	0
Glynis	40	0	0	0	0	0	0	0	0	0	0	0	0
Katie	10	0	0	0	0	0	0	0	0	0	0	0	0
Jordan	34	0	0	0	0	0	0	0	0	0	0	0	0
Jessica	62	0	0	0	0	0	0	0	0	0	0	0	0
Andrew	37	0	0	0	0	0	0	0	0	0	0	0	0
Ricky	56	0	0	0	0	0	0	0	0	0	0	0	0
Paula	94	0	0	0	0	0	0	0	0	0	0	0	0
Felice	45	0	0	0	0	0	0	0	0	2.22	0	2.22	0
All subjects	500	0	0.13	0.39	0	0.53	0	0	0.13	0.22	0	0.35	0

subjects, seven produced more target than non-target combinations, indicating that training might indeed be affecting the production of relational combinations and also that the production of sequences and of combinations may be different phenomena which are affected differently by manipulation of the verbal environment.

Examples provided by adults during the training period

Table 25 shows the number of examples of each target and non-target relation which were presented during the training and follow-up session. Entries in table 25 are actual counts of examples rather than percentages since it was impossible to calculate the total percentage of adult speech which was devoted to training. It should be remembered that all counts were based on the sampling procedure, which represented about 20 per cent of the actual experimental procedure, so the counts should be multiplied by approximately five in order to obtain the total number of examples involved over the entire training period. Little comment is required. The table indicates that most direct training involved the three target relations, as expected. The number of examples of each relation provided to each subject varied as a result of the experimenter following the subject's lead during training, as described in chapter 3. This also led to the provision of examples for non-target relations. As table 25 also indicates, although examples were presented, as planned in both complete grammatical, or 'adult' form and shortened or 'child' form, there were generally more adult-form examples. Table 22, which shows parallel figures for the observation period, is included to provide a base line against which to judge the intensity of the training procedure. 'Training' situations were avoided whenever possible during the observation period; nevertheless, some examples of relations were provided.

Although the training procedure has been described in detail in chapter 3, some illustrations of the types of examples provided by adults might be helpful. The following segment, which demonstrates training of the locative relation, is taken from the final session with Lia. Lia's mother had drawn a picture of a fish on a piece of paper. Suddenly, Lia grabbed the experimenter's note-paper and began looking on and under each sheet. The sequence here begins after the experimenter had tried to ask Lia about ownership of a toy truck. 'Bish' is Lia's word for fish, and 'baa' for bath or fishbowl.

TABLE 24 *Number of examples of each relation presented by all adults present: observation period*

S	Subject–verb-object			Locative			Possessive			'I want'			Negative			Salutes			Other		
	A	C	T	A	C	T	A	C	T	A	C	T	A	C	T	A	C	T	A	C	T
Lia	0	0	0	0	0	0	3	0	3	0	0	0	0	0	0	0	0	0	1	0	1
Deanna	1	0	1	1	1	2	0	3	3	0	0	0	0	0	0	0	0	0	1	0	1
Glynis	0	0	0	0	0	0	0	0	0	0	0	0	0	0	0	0	0	0	1	0	1
Katie	4	0	4	0	8	8	2	2	4	0	0	0	0	0	0	0	0	0	3	0	3
Jordan	9	1	10	0	10	10	9	1	10	0	0	0	0	0	0	10	2	12	6	0	6
Jessica	1	18	19	0	0	0	0	0	0	0	0	0	0	0	0	3	0	3	3	13	16
Andrew	0	0	0	0	0	0	0	0	0	0	0	0	0	0	0	0	0	0	1	0	1
Ricky	0	0	0	0	0	0	0	0	0	0	0	0	0	0	0	0	0	0	0	0	0
Paula	3	0	3	0	0	0	0	0	0	0	0	0	0	0	0	0	0	0	2	0	2
Felice	0	0	0	1	0	1	0	0	0	0	0	0	0	0	0	4	0	4	0	0	0

A = examples presented in 'adult' form, complete, correct English, e.g. 'It's Mommy's hat.'
C = examples presented in 'child' or shortened form, e.g. 'Mommy hat'.
T = total number of examples presented for a relation, including both 'adult' and 'child' forms.

TABLE 25 *Number of examples of each relation presented by all adults present: training and follow-up period*

S	Subject–verb–object			Locative			Possessive			'I want'			Negative			Salutes			Other		
	A	C	T	A	C	T	A	C	T	A	C	T	A	C	T	A	C	T	A	C	T
Lia	8	3	11	23	14	37	50	12	62	0	0	0	0	0	0	27	3	30	56	33	89
Deanna	56	15	71	15	21	36	6	6	12	4	0	4	1	0	1	1	0	1	11	4	15
Glynis	16	11	27	12	12	24	17	3	20	2	2	4	3	0	3	25	0	25	9	16	25
Katie	14	4	18	14	7	21	13	1	14	8	1	9	2	0	2	1	0	1	0	0	0
Jordan	32	13	45	6	10	16	10	0	10	0	0	0	0	0	0	10	0	10	12	13	25
Jessica	65	20	85	4	0	4	50	8	58	10	10	20	0	0	0	5	0	5	21	25	46
Andrew	15	4	19	2	7	9	9	0	9	0	0	0	0	0	0	0	0	0	6	17	23
Ricky	33	5	38	7	7	14	30	7	37	0	0	0	0	0	0	16	0	16	6	10	16
Paula	25	14	39	6	6	12	46	27	73	0	0	0	0	0	0	2	0	2	8	2	10
Felice	67	13	80	3	4	7	33	4	37	0	0	0	0	0	0	3	0	3	4	3	7

A = Examples presented in 'adult form', complete, correct English, e.g. 'It's Mommy's hat.'

C = Examples presented in 'child' or shortened form, e.g. 'Mommy hat'.

T = Total number of examples presented for a relation, including both 'adult' and 'child' forms.

E:	Whose truck is that, Lia?	mm ba
	Whose is it?	mm bish
		mm bish
E:	Where's the fish?	mm mm bish
M:	No, no honey (the mother thinks the subject is disturbing the experimenter's note-taking).	mm bish (She is looking under paper.)
		mm mm bish
M:	She's looking for the fish on the paper.	
E:	Oh, that fish. *Where is the fish?*	
	Can you say *fish on the paper?*	mm bish
		mm jish
		mm mm oo ha
		mm joo (followed by babbling)
E:	Lia, *where's that fish?*	
M:	Fish?	
E:	*Where's the fish,* Lia?	uh baa! (points to fish-bowl in room)
E:	Good girl!	
M:	In the bath?	
E:	*Fish bath*	mm bish (looking on paper)
		mm bish
		mm bish

In the above excerpt, 'fish on the paper' (no verb) and 'fish bath' were both counted as examples given in abbreviated, child-like form. Questions of the type, 'Where is the fish?' were used extensively as described in chapter 3, but are not counted as training examples.

A typical example of a subject–verb relation, here with no object, is taken from Ricky's second training session:

E:	(Clock is ticking very loud and the experimenter thinks Ricky is listening to it.)	
	Do you see the clock?	no
		cock (=clock)
		cock

E: Say yes.   cock
E: *Clock ticks.*   cock
                                       no (simultaneously, as the
                                           experimenter provides
                                           example)

'Clock ticks' is an example provided in full, correct, adult form.

Possessive examples were short and straightforward. For example, during Paula's second training session, Paula looked at a picture of a duck with a nest of eggs and said: 'egg'. The experimenter said, *'Duck egg. It's the duck's egg'*, providing both full-form and child-form examples.

In table 26, the percentages of target sequences and combinations are compared to the total number of examples of each relation provided by adults. There does not appear to be any simple relation between the number of examples and either sequential or combinatorial expression.

Additional information: responses to questions and widely-separated sequences

Table 27 presents the additional information pertaining to the understanding of linguistic relations, the responses to questions and instances of widely-separated sequences of holophrases.

All subjects now provide some examples of relationally correct answers to questions; the percentages of the subjects' total speech range from about 2 per cent to about 7 per cent. Six subjects now provide a very few examples of widely separated 'sequences' of holophrases, 1 per cent or less. An example of a correct response to a question was provided in the preceding section in which the experimenter asked, 'Where's the fish?' and Lia answered, 'uh baa!' (bath). A widely separated sequence consists of two utterances separated by an interval of several seconds, which would have been considered to be a relational combination or sequence had they been uttered more closely together.

PSYCHOLINGUISTIC CHANGES OVER THE COURSE OF THE STUDY:
FROM OBSERVATION TO TRAINING AND FOLLOW-UP SESSIONS

One major portion of this study was an attempt to produce changes in the subjects' single-word and combinatorial speech. The goal was to enable the subject to express via two-word combinations relations which he was assumed to be expressing holophrastically. Changes in the pattern of holophrastic and non-holophrastic single-word speech as well as changes

TABLE 26 *Number of examples of each target relation presented by adults compared to percentage of sequences and combinations produced by each subject during the training period* [a]

S	Subject–verb–object			Locative			Possessive		
	No. adult examples	% Sequences	% Combinations	No. adult examples	% Sequences	% Combinations	No. adult examples	% Sequences	% Combinations
Lia	11	0	0.20	33	0	0.62	62	0.20	0
Deanna	61	0.79	0.19	30	0	0	10	0.19	0
Glynis	23	0	0	24	1.02	0.34	10	0	0.68
Katie	13	1.90	4.76	21	0	0	12	0	0
Jordan	44	0	2.33	14	0.93	0.46	6	0	0.93
Jessica	70	0	2.00	4	0	0.83	46	0	0.66
Andrew	17	0	0	8	0	0	7	0	0.56
Ricky	30	0	1.14	9	0	0	31	0	0.28
Paula	25	0	0	12	0	0	50	0	0
Felice	62	1.85	6.19	3	0	0	35	0	0
All subjects	356	0.45	1.68	158	0.20	0.23	269	0.04	0.33

[a] These figures include the total number of examples provided by adults in both adult and child form for the training sessions only. (Follow-up session is excluded from this table.)

TABLE 27   *Correct response to questions, and widely separated sequences during training and follow-up period (expressed in percentages of each subject's single-word speech)*

Subject	No. utt.	Response to questions	Separated sequences
Lia	542	4	1
Deanna	547	5	0
Glynis	322	5	0
Katie	109	3	1 (0.95)
Jordan	235	2	1 (0.87)
Jessica	346	7	1 (0.57)
Andrew	204	7	0
Ricky	381	6	0 (0.26)
Paula	331	7	0 (0.30)
Felice	233	7	0
All subjects	3250	5	0 (0.30)

in the pattern of sequences of holophrases and true two-word combinations should show the effects of the intervention procedures.

Changes in the pattern of holophrastic and non-holophrastic single-word speech

Tables 9 and 16 present the patterns of holophrastic and non-holophrastic speech for the observation period, and for the training and follow-up sessions respectively. Considering the total proportion of holophrastic and non-holophrastic speech, one notices that during the training and follow-up period the distribution of holophrastic speech has shifted slightly upward, and the range has become narrower. A Wilcoxon matched-pairs, signed-ranks test was not significant, however, indicating that although four subjects increased in amount of holophrastic speech, and six subjects decreased, the overall distribution remained approximately the same.[1]

[1] A series of Wilcoxon tests were carried out on the group of ten subjects to determine training effects for the group as a whole. It should be noted again, however, that such group treatment necessarily obscures individual differences. The fact that there are or are not significant differences for the entire group speaks to the issue of efficacy of training, *assuming* that training has the same, or similar, functional effects across subjects. In the case of a process such as language acquisition which may perhaps take different forms in different children, such group analysis could be less important than an individual assessment of change in each subject. It must be remembered, however, that at the time this study was planned, this issue was far from settled. Up until this time, there had been no group analyses of as many as ten single-word subjects. It was therefore considered necessary that *both* group and individual analyses be included, and that neither should a priori be considered more appropriate than the other. Lack of statistical significance in group tests, however, does *not* mean that there are no important individual effects.

In the case of the three target holophrases, subject–verb–object, locatives, and possessives, Wilcoxon tests were again non-significant in all three cases, indicating that the over-all distribution remained approximately the same, with some subjects increasing and some decreasing the proportion of holophrastic expression of each relation. One should note, however, that there was generally more expression of both the locative and possessive relations during the training period. Five subjects provided locative examples during training and follow-up as opposed to four subjects during observation; two of these subjects had also provided locative examples during observation. Eight subjects provided examples of the possessive relation, including the two subjects who had done so during observation. Again, as during the observation period, many more subject–verb–object holophrases were expressed than either of the other two target relations. It is also noteworthy that six subjects either increased or decreased their holophrastic expression of the subject–verb–object relationship by more than 10 per cent. The pattern of utterances is not the same during training and observation; perhaps this pattern is affected by the different verbal 'climate' provided by the adults in the environment.

Changes in the pattern of expression of non-target holophrases are also of interest. In general, the trend was similar to that for target holophrases. Some subjects showed an increase, and some a decrease, for each relation. In all cases except the negative holophrase, Wilcoxon tests were non-significant. The proportion of negative holophrases did substantially increase during the training and follow-up period; $p < 0.05$, two-tailed. This is probably a result of, or a reaction to, the training procedure with its emphasis on verbal production.

While there was no significant change in the over-all pattern of non-holophrastic utterances, nor in the 'naming' or 'other' categories, the proportion of repetitions did increase significantly during training and follow-up ($p < 0.02$, two-tailed), probably as a result of the training procedure which directly encouraged repetition. As has already been noted, Paula, the subject who produced the highest proportion of repetitions during training, also produced the lowest proportion of total holophrastic utterances, and also decreased in proportion of holophrastic speech from observation to training.

Changes in the proportion of two-word sequences and two-word combinations

Considering first, the 'pseudo-combinations', i.e. combinations of non-meaningful sounds with meaningful words, one compares tables 13 and 18 for the observation, and training and follow-up periods respectively. It is apparent that some subjects slightly increased and some subjects decreased their production in all three categories, 'mm', 'uh', and 'other sounds'. None of the changes in distributions is significant, although the production of 'other sounds + words' did tend to decrease during the training and follow-up period; the Wilcoxon test approached significance at the 0.05 level.

In order to determine whether the proportion of two-word combinations increased as a result of the training procedure, one must consider tables 11 for the observation period, 20 for the training period, and 22 for the follow-up session. Comparing the results obtained during the observation and training period by means of the Wilcoxon signed-ranks, matched-pairs test, one finds that there are no significant differences between the patterns of total relational and non-relational two-word combinations produced during these two periods. There is also no significant difference in the 'other' relations, linguistic relations which were not specific targets of the training procedure. The picture is different, however, for the three target relations, subject–verb–object, locatives, and possessives. The subject–verb–object relation shows a tendency to increase during the training period, although this tendency is not significant. On the locative and possessive relations, however, several subjects increased, and no subjects decreased, so the increase is significant, $p < 0.01$, two-tailed, for both relations. One should be cautious in interpreting these results, since many subjects began observation not expressing one or the other of these relations at all, and since the actual magnitude of these differences is small, in all cases less than 1 per cent of total intelligible utterances. On the other hand, as has been said repeatedly, even a small increase may well indicate that verbal production can be affected by the type of verbal interaction provided by adults.

When considering changes in the number of combinations from the training period to the follow-up session, one must remember that a much smaller number of utterances is involved for the follow-up session. An apparent increase in the total number of relational combinations is not significant. On the other hand, no non-relational combinations were expressed by any subject during the follow-up session. There were no significant differences in the expression of any of the three target relations, although only one subject, Felice, produced any examples of the possessive relationship during the follow-up session. For practical purposes, the pattern during the follow-up session is similar to an individual training session selected at random.

Although the training procedure was directly concerned with increasing the number of two-word combinations, one might expect a complementary increase in any steps intermediate to the expression of combinations, such as sequences of holophrases. Again, the relevant data appear in tables 11, 20, and 22. There is no significant difference in the pattern for all relational sequences of holophrases. There is a significant increase in the number of non-relational sequences of holophrases, $p < 0.05$, although again the magnitude of difference is extremely small; the largest increase is 1 per cent for Ricky. There is no significant difference in the expression of sequences of holophrases among relations which were not targets of the training procedure. There were also no significant differences for any of the three target relations, subject–verb–object, locatives, or possessives. The total number of sequences expressing these three relations remained extremely small.

Comparing the proportion of sequences expressed during training and during the follow-up session, one again notes that there were very few sequences produced during the follow-up sessions. Nevertheless, none of the differences, for over-all patterns of relational and non-relational sequences, or for specific relations, is significant. Again, the follow-up session appears similar to a training session. Further, as table 24 indicates, there is no apparent relation between the number of training examples provided by adults and the number of sequences of holophrases and two-word combinations produced by the subject.

There is one further point regarding the effectiveness of the training procedures. If one were successful in training a subject in expressing in two words a relation which he had previously been expressing holophrastically, one might expect the holophrastic expression of this relation to decrease as the two-word expression increased and replaced single-word expression. As noted, there was a significant, although extremely small increase in two-word expression of the possessive and locative relations during the training period. It has also been noted in the preceding section, however, that there was no significant decrease in holophrastic expression of these two relations for the group as a whole. Looking at individual cases, only Lia very slightly decreased her holophrastic expression of locatives, and Lia, Glynis, Jessica, and Ricky very slightly decreased expression of possessives. Other subjects, however, slightly increased holophrastic expression, or showed no change. For subject–verb–object expression, of seven subjects who increased expression of combinations, four had decreased holophrastic expression and three increased. While there is an increase in patterned speech during training, then, there is no clear pattern relating increase in sequential or combinatorial expression of a particular relation to change in proportion of holophrastic expression.

Responses to questions, and widely separated sequences

The last data indicating whether the subjects understood linguistic relations is concerned with the correct answers to questions, and the occurrence of widely separated sequences. Comparing tables 15 and 27 for the observation, and training and follow-up periods, respectively, one notes that there is a significant increase in the number of correct answers to questions, $p < 0.05$ two-tailed, although again the differences are of the magnitude of about 2 per cent. There is no significant difference in the occurrence of widely separated sequences of holophrases.

Summary of psycholinguistic data

The classification system used in this study revealed regularities in the single-word speech of ten subjects under two verbal environmental conditions: relatively naturalistic observation, and an interventive training situation. Changes in the pattern under these two conditions were also evident, both for individual subjects and for the group as a whole.

Using this system, there is substantial evidence for the phenomenon of holophrastic, or relational single-word speech. During the observation period, eight of ten subjects used 40 per cent or more of their speech holophrastically; during training, nine of ten subjects did so. Other large proportions of single-word speech were interpreted as simple naming, and as repetition, or imitation of an adult's preceding utterance. There is some suggestion that the subjects who do the most repeating or imitating also show the lowest proportion of holophrastic expression

The most common relation expressed holophrastically by these subjects is 'I want'. Of the three target relations, subject–verb–object, locatives, and possessives, the subject–verb–object relation was expressed most often, and by the largest number of subjects. The pattern of holophrastic expression for individual subjects changed from observation to training. The only statistically significant changes for the group as a whole were an increase in the proportion of negative holophrases, and an increase in the proportion of repetitions.

Most subjects produced small numbers of sequences of holophrases, as well as small numbers of true two-word combinations throughout the course of the study. By and large, these relations appeared in the customary word order in which they appear in adult English, although a very few 'inverted' sequences and combinations appeared throughout the study. Again, there were changes in patterned speech, specifically increases in combinatorial expression of the three target relations for individual subjects. The increase in the combinatorial expression of the locative and possessive relations was statistically significant for the group of ten subjects. The magnitude of change was small. There was also a significant increase in the number of relationally correct answers to questions.

COMPARISON OF SENSORY-MOTOR ABILITIES AND PSYCHOLINGUISTIC ABILITIES

Another major goal of this study was the clarification of the relation between sensory-motor abilities and psycholinguistic abilities at the end of the single-word period in language acquisition. A summary of the results of the sensory-motor tests and the level of psycholinguistic ability for each subject during the observation period is presented in table 28. This table is useful in assessing both the over-all abilities of this group of subjects, and the individual pattern of abilities for each subject.

It is obvious from table 28 that there is no simple pattern of sensory-motor abilities which characterizes the ten subjects in this study. Most subjects differ widely across both sensory-motor and psycholinguistic tasks. There is no indication that sensory-motor ability as measured by these tasks, varies directly or inversely with level of psycholinguistic performance as assessed here. It is apparent that some of these tests, particularly those measuring role playing may have been too difficult, since the response to them was so poor. Finally, because of the varying scoring systems used for the sensory-motor tests, it is impossible to compare the group's performance statistically on sensory-motor and psycholinguistic 'correlates' to a relation. It is, however, possible to do this on an individual basis, and this comparison is included in the individual analysis which follows. Considering each subject individually, the differences in patterns of abilities are striking.

Lia

Due to her refusal to co-operate on several sensory-motor tasks, and the unintentional omission of the displacement series, Lia's sensory-motor data is incomplete. She performs at the lowest level, pairing, on the stacking-cups task. On the other hand, she provides examples both of symbolic play and of deferred imitation. In contrast to the stacking-cups task, these are abilities which have been proven by Piaget and his associates to be associated with the close of the sensory-motor period. On the psycholinguistic side, Lia is generally quite advanced. Like the other subjects, she did not show any clear preference in obeying either child-form or well-formed commands. She did, however, show a high proportion of holophrastic speech, 56 per cent, as well as 2 per cent relational sequences of holophrases. She was not yet, however, producing any two-word combinations. Comparing her primitive performance on the stacking-cups task to its linguistic correlate, one finds in table 9 that 21 per cent of Lia's single-word utterances were examples of the subject–verb–object relation. Lia also provided examples of both the locative and possessive relations.

Deanna

Deanna demonstrated the ability to use one object to act upon another, although she did not reverse this task. On the stacking-cups task, she was advanced, producing mostly pots, but providing examples of all three types of structures. On the linguistic correlate to these two abilities, the subject–verb–object relation, table 9 indicates that Deanna expressed this relation in 34 per cent of her single-word utterances, by far the largest percentage in this category for any subject. Deanna could perform the minimal, single visible displacement, and she could mimic an action immediately after its presentation. She did not provide any examples of symbolic play or role playing; there was one spontaneous example of deferred imitation.

Again, Deanna shows no preference in the types of commands obeyed. She is as yet producing no two-word combinations, although she produces some sequences of holophrases, both relational and non-relational. Her proportion of holophrastic utterances, 69 per cent, is the highest in the study. She can also answer a few questions correctly, and produces a few separated sequences. Although she can perform a single visible displacement, she provides no examples of the linguistic correlate, the locative relation.

Glynis

Glynis shows perhaps the most advanced over-all pattern of abilities in both the sensory-motor and verbal areas. She can use one object to act upon

TABLE 28 *Summary of sensory-motor and psycholinguistic abilities during the observation period*

S	Act.-obj.		Stacking-cups task			Sensory-motor						Imitation	
						Displacement				Symbolic play	Role play		
						Visible		Invisible					
	Fd.	Rev.	% Pr.	% Pots	% Sub.	1	2	1	2			Immediate	Deferred
Lia	N.A.	N.A.	100	0	0	N.A.	N.A.	N.A.	N.A.	+	0	–	+
Deanna	+	–	33.3	58.3	8.3	+	–	–	–	0	0	+	+
Glynis	+	+	63.1	36.8	0	+	+	+	+^{c}	+	0	0	+
Katie	0	–	45.5	45.5	9.0	+	0	0	0	0	0	0	0
Jordan	0	0	83.3	16.7	0	+	+	–	0	+	0	+	+
Jessica	+	+	69.5	17.3	13.0	+	+	0	0	+	+	0	+
Andrew	+	+	100	0	0	N.A.	N.A.	N.A.	N.A.	+	0	+	+
Ricky	0	0	100	0	0	+	+	0	0	+	0	0	0
Paula	+	+	33.3	66.7	0	+	+	+	0	+	0	+	+
Felice	+	+	50.0	33.3	16.7	+	0	0	0	+	–	+	+

	Form preference		% Sequences of holophrases[a]		% Two-word combinations[a]		Psycholinguistic		
S	Ch.	Well	Rel.	Non-rel.	Rel.	Non-rel.	% Holophrasic[b]	% Questions[b]	% Sep. seq.[b]
Lia	4	4	2.23	0.55	0	0	57	0.55	0.55
Deanna	3	4	0.70	0.35	0	0	69	1	2
Glynis	3	3	3.96	0	1.98	0	64	4	0
Katie	4	4	0.63	0	0.56	0	29	0	0
Jordan	1	2	0	1.12	1.12	0	29	3	0
Jessica	3	6	0.53	0	1.60	0.53	44	2	0
Andrew	5	4	0.55	0	1.65	0	49	1	0
Ricky	5	4	1.24	1.24	3.73	3.32	54	2	0
Paula	3	3	0.60	0.91	0.60	0	40	0	0
Felice	2	4	0.85	0	13.56	0.85	44	3	0

+ Indicates successful completion of a task, at least once.
− Indicates failure to successfully complete a task.
o Indicates refusal to attempt a task.
N.A. Indicates task not administered.
Act.-obj. = test in which the subject must use one object to act upon another.
Fd. = forward direction – initial task.
Rev. = reverse of forward task.
Pr. = pairing structures.
Pots = pot structures.
Sub. = sub-assembly structures (see text).
Ch. = child-form commands (see text).
Well = complete commands.
Rel. = relational.
Non-rel. = non-relational
Sep. seq. = widely separated sequences of holophrases.
Questions = subject's correct response to questions.
[a] Expressed in percentages of each subject's single-word plus combinatorial speech.
[b] Expressed in percentages of each subject's single-word speech.
[c] Administered two weeks after Glynis's final follow-up session.

another, and she can reverse the task. On the stacking-cups series, she is intermediate between the pairing and pot structures, although she produces no sub-assemblies. Two weeks after the close of the study, she can successfully complete the entire displacement series. She also provides examples of deferred imitation, even though she will not mimic immediately. She gave no examples of role playing ability. Although she did well on the sensory-motor correlates, table 9 indicates, however, that Glynis produced only 4 per cent examples of the subject—verb—object relationship, and no examples of locatives. Glynis's total proportion of holophrastic utterances was high, 64 per cent and she produced the most correct responses to questions. She showed some tendency to produce relational sequences and combinations, at the same time producing no sequences or combinations which are non-relational.

Katie

Katie showed mixed dominance on the stacking-cups task, illustrating all three strategies. She was also able to perform a single visible displacement. Table 9 indicates that her correlate linguistic abilities were not present; she showed only 4 per cent holophrastic expression for subject—verb—object, and no examples of locatives. Katie did not succeed on any other sensory-motor task. She showed no preference in obeying commands. Her proportion of holophrastic utterances was very low, 29 per cent. She did produce a few relational sequences and combinations, and no non-relational sequences and combinations.

Jordan

Jordan showed mixed dominance on the stacking-cups task, producing mostly pairs, some pots, and no sub-assemblies; he did not succeed in using one object to act upon another. Table 9 indicates that he produced 9 per cent holophrastic examples of the subject—verb—object relation, the correlate to these abilities. He successfully performed single and double visible displacement, while he produced no examples of the linguistic locative relation. He gave examples of immediate and deferred imitation, as well as of symbolic play. Like the other subjects, he provided no examples of role playing. Jordan's proportion of holophrastic speech was very low, 29 per cent. He produced no relational sequences, but some non-relational sequences. He also produced some simple relational combinations, such as 'Hi Jenny'. Jordan obeyed only three commands.

Jessica

Jessica showed the most advanced over-all sensory-motor pattern. She showed mixed dominance on the stacking-cups task, with all three strategies included. The only thing she did not do were invisible displacements, and immediate mimicking of an action. She was the only subject to provide examples of role playing, in this case, 'Mommy washing the clothes'. Jessica was one of the few subjects to demonstrate a preference in obeying commands; she responded 2:1 in favor of adult forms. Jessica's proportion of holophrastic speech was 44 per cent. She produced a few relational sequences, and no non-relational sequences. She also produced some relational combinations and a smaller number of non-relational combinations. She could answer some questions correctly. Table 9 indicates that her correlate subject–verb–object expression was high, 23 per cent, but she provided no examples of locatives.

Andrew

Andrew's sensory-motor data is incomplete. He could use one object to act upon another, and could reverse this task. On the stacking-cups task, however, he produced only a few pairs. He provided examples of symbolic play, and immediate and deferred imitation, but would attempt no other sensory-motor tasks. Table 9 indicates that his subject–verb–object expression was fairly high, 9 per cent, and he also produced 0.55 per cent locative holophrases. His proportion of holophrastic utterances was 49 per cent. He produced some relational sequences and combinations, and no non-relational sequences and combinations. He answered a small number of questions correctly, and showed no clear preference in obeying commands.

Ricky

Ricky's sensory-motor performance was generally poor. He produced only two primitive pairing structures for stacking cups. He successfully performed single and double visible displacements, and he demonstrated symbolic play, but would attempt no other tasks. He showed no preference in obeying commands. Table 9 indicates that in contrast Ricky exhibited a high proportion of subject–verb–object holophrases, 16 per cent, although there were no locative holophrases. His proportion of holophrastic speech was high, 54 per cent. He produced several examples of sequences and two-word combinations, both relational and non-relational. He answered a few questions correctly.

Paula

Paula appeared to be uniformly advanced on sensory-motor skills. She could use one object to act upon another, and could reverse this. On the stacking-cups task, she showed mixed dominance, definitely tending toward pots, although she produced no sub-assemblies. She succeeded at all displacements except two invisible displacements. She provided examples of symbolic play, and immediate and deferred imitation. Paula also provided linguistic examples of both correlate relations, 8 per cent subject–verb–object holophrases, and 0.3 per cent locatives, as shown in table 9. Her percentage of holophrastic speech was 40 per cent. She produced a few relational sequences and combinations. She also produced some non-relational sequences, actually more than the relational ones.

Felice

Felice was able to use one object to act upon another, and to demonstrate an advanced pattern using all three strategies on the stacking-cups task. Her linguistic correlate to these abilities was fairly high, 12 per cent, shown in table 9. She succeeded only at one visible displacement, yet she produced a few, 1 per cent, locative holophrases. She provided examples of symbolic play, and she could mimic an action immediately. She provided spontaneous examples of deferred imitation. She attempted, but failed the role playing task. Felice produced 45 per cent holophrastic utterances. She produced a few relational sequences, and a few non-relational combinations. Her proportion of two-word combinations was exceptionally high, 13.56 per cent, and she could answer a few questions.

Again considering the linguistic and cognitive correlate tasks for all subjects, there is no readily apparent pattern. Some subjects who did well on the cognitive tasks, also showed high proportions of holophrastic uses of the correlate relations. On the other hand, some showed extremely low proportions. The same is true for the subjects who did poorly on the cognitive tasks. In short, these data do not support the notion that the subject–verb–object relation is a true correlate of either the stacking-cups task or the ability to use one object to act upon another, or the notion that the ability to succeed in the displacement series is a correlate of the locative relation.

In order to shed some light on the relationship between over-all sensory-motor and psycholinguistic level, the subjects who were least advanced in sensory-motor performance as shown in table 28, were compared to the five more advanced subjects. There was no relation to increase or decrease in target or non-target holophrases, or increase or decrease in relational and non-relational sequences and combinations. Reversing this procedure, and considering the four subjects who showed the greatest increase in relational combinations, Katie, Jordan, Jessica, and Andrew (as revealed in tables 11 and 20), there was no consistent relation to any of the sensory motor measures.

Summary of the comparison of sensory-motor and psycholinguistic data

There was no clear-cut pattern of sensory-motor abilities which characterized these subjects and which could be compared to the pattern of psycholinguistic abilities. There was no evidence to support the notion that any of the proposed correlates to linguistic abilities were in fact related, as measured by the level of ability achieved on the tasks as presented in this study. On the other hand, based upon the tests of symbolic play and deferred imitation, most subjects appear to have completed, or almost completed the sensory-motor stage of cognitive development. It is true that only one subject succeeded at the role playing task, but this is a skill which only has its roots in the sensory-motor period, and is not mastered until much later. The only task which does not consistently appear to be mastered at the usual level at the end of sensory-motor development is the displacement series. According to Piaget's data, described in previous chapters, these subjects should have been able successfully to retrieve an object after two invisible displacements. Most subjects were, however, able to retrieve an object after a single visible displacement, which was the minimal ability proposed as the correlate to the locative relation in this study. The theoretical implications of the subjects' cognitive and psycholinguistic performance will now be discussed.

5 Toward a theory of single-word usage

As described in chapter 2, there were three goals of this study. The first was to demonstrate that there is an identifiable phenomenon of holophrastic usage, i.e. patterns and structure in single-word speech analogous to linguistic relations. This involved devising a classification system which would reveal regularities across a large number of children, despite the well-known fact that acquisition patterns vary greatly from child to child. Using this system, it was necessary to show that holophrasis is not an infrequent phenomenon, but rather represents a substantial proportion of these children's single-word speech, and for this reason can be assumed to be of significance in the acquisition process. It will be hypothesized that the appearance of underlying linguistic relations at the very beginning of language development is one indication of the essential continuity between single-word and combinatorial speech.

Once holophrastic usage was demonstrated to exist, the second aspect of the study was an attempt to train children who were currently expressing certain linguistic relations holophrastically to express these same relations by means of two-word combinations. This attempt involved the additional assumption that it is possible to train patterns in language acquisition, i.e. speed up the usual rate of acquisition. Finally, the third goal was the investigation and clarification of the relationship between psycholinguistic abilities at this period and cognitive, or sensory-motor abilities. In order to answer this question, it was necessary to depend both upon the children's spontaneous demonstrations of their cognitive abilities and to devise special tests to measure both their general level of representational ability, and specific skills which were assumed to be 'correlates' to certain linguistic relations.

In order to determine whether and how these goals have been met, this chapter will be organized around five basic issues:

1. Based upon this sample of ten children, does there appear to be evidence that holophrastic usage is an important phenomenon in single-word

speech? What is the function of holophrastic usage? How much individual variation is there?

2. Was it possible to train a child who was holophrastically expressing a relation to express the same relation by means of a two-word combination?

3. What appears to be necessary to move a child out of the holophrastic period?

4. What information does this study provide about the relationship between language development during the single-word period and cognitive or sensory-motor development?

5. In summary, on the basis of this study, how should one characterize the single-word period of language acquisition? What is the relationship between the single-word period and later language acquisition? In the process of discussing these five issues, it will be necessary to deal with several methodological and theoretical issues involved in the design and execution of the study itself.

What evidence does this study provide for the existence
and function of holophrases?

Using the classification system described in chapter 3, it was possible to divide all ten children's single-word speech into holophrastic and non-holophrastic categories. Again, for purposes of this study a holophrase was defined as the child's use of a single word to convey something like the meaning which an adult will usually convey through the use of a linguistic relation involving more than one word. A holophrase does not necessarily convey the meaning of an entire adult sentence. The 'relations' defined here can be consistently identified in adult speech, but they were not drawn from any one existing system of linguistic classification. In order to classify these single-word utterances as holophrastic or non-holophrastic, it was necessary to utilize the extralinguistic context of the utterance. As discussed in chapters 1 and 2, one justification for the use of such procedures is the fact that it produces a stable and reliable classification system, which permits the identification of consistent regularities and patterns in child speech. Such a system was obtained here.

Using this classification, substantial proportions of all ten children's speech were classifiable as holophrastic. In eight of ten cases during observation, and nine of ten cases during training, 40 per cent or more of the child's single-word speech could be understood in this manner. This is ample evidence that holophrastic usage is a solid phenomenon during the single-word period, although it by no means encompasses all of the child's verbal production at this time. Other processes, particularly naming and considerable repetition of adult utterances are occurring simultaneously. One obvious explanation would be that the three verbal mechanisms are indicative of three underlying processes during this phase of language acquisition. Each concerns a separate aspect of the acquisition of a shared arbitrary communication system; each, therefore, serves an important and separate function during the single-word period.

In this analysis, holophrastic usage represents the first steps in the child's progress toward an understanding of linguistic relations, syntactic and semantic, in the adult sense. The possibility of describing holophrastic usage in terms similar to those which describe relations present in adult speech suggests an underlying continuity of development from the holophrastic through the combinatorial periods. The consistent use of a single word to express a linguistic relation appears to be the beginning of the child's attempt both to conceptualize the relations exemplified by the language system in use in his environment, and also to learn to express these same relations in the most efficient way.

In this scheme, naming involves the child's linking of the cognitive idea that different objects exist with the accepted verbal means of representing those objects in his culture. The child's cognitive development should have reached the point where he is aware that permanent objects exist separate from himself, and that there are many different objects, all of which retain their basic properties despite his various manipulations with them, and all of which have certain identifying characteristics. Naming, then, represents the child's attempt to classify efficiently the objects in the world around him, or perhaps more accurately, to discover the classification system which is in use in his particular environment.

The third process, repetition, or imitation involves the child's acquisition of the shared sound patterns and vocabulary items which the other persons around the child are already using to communicate with one another, as well as with the child. It has been commonly believed, although without systematic investigation upon which to base this claim, that imitation must play a major role in language acquisition. It is well-known that children begin language acquisition by babbling, i.e. using sounds which do not have a shared meaning in their communities; often later they devise words of their own. Through some process which must include some form of covert imitation or overt repetition they eventually adopt the standard terms and gradually drop these 'baby talk' equivalents.

Learning theory accounts (Mowrer, 1960; Bijou & Baer, 1965) attempted to explain most of language acquisition as a gradual process of the child's matching his verbal productions to those in use in the community around him. Although it has been consistently shown (Chomsky, 1957, 1965; McNeill, 1966, 1970b; Brown, 1973) that syntax cannot be acquired in this fashion, sound patterns and vocabulary items particular to any one language can, and indeed must be, imitated. This material is openly available to the child, and he can actively process it to produce utterances similar to those produced by others around him. In this analysis, then, repetition or imitation plays an important role in the accumulation of vocabulary items, and one would expect to find a large amount of imitation among children just beginning to use single words.

At the same time, overt repetition may indicate the child's awareness of yet another aspect of language, the fact that language is a communication system, a means by which one person can make his internal states, needs, and wishes known to another person through the use of a shared arbitrary system of symbols. In repeating, the child makes an early attempt at dyadic communicative interaction. He has received a message, and he responds by sending a similar message of his own. He must be aware then, both of the alternating speaker–listener relationship which calls for responses on his part to utterances made by others, and of the need for the symbols he uses to match those used by others around him, in order to communicate efficiently.

If these three processes are understood as necessary for the child's eventual communication with those around him, and if evidence such as the results of this study is accepted as indicating that all three processes are occurring during the same time span, then one would not expect either that the occurrence of holophrastic usages precludes the occurrence of other mechanisms such as naming, or that all, or even the majority of a child's single-word speech must be holophrastic in order to assume that the phenomenon of holophrastic speech is 'real'. Indeed, in this scheme holophrastic usage serves a specific function, the first expression of syntactic and semantic relations. But this is only one of three important functions involved in the acquisition of language, and one would not expect all of single-word speech to be concerned with just this one aspect. All ten children in this study used at least 29 per cent of their single-word speech holophrastically during the observation period. This represents a substantial proportion of the total utterances, and should be more than enough to indicate that this phenomenon is real.

The large range in the proportion of holophrastic usage among the ten children, from about 29 per cent to about 69 per cent during the observation period, should call attention to the individual nature of language acquisition, and the possibility that different children may adopt alternate functional strategies or approaches to the problem of language acquisition. Many previous investigators (Bloom, 1970; Brown, 1973; Smith, 1970; Greenfield et al., in press; Nelson, 1973) have noted large individual differences in the patterns of speech presented by different children at various early stages of language acquisition. The discovery of individual differences at this very earliest stage lends support to the notion that there are optional paths to the same endpoint, and that these strategic differences operate from the very outset of the process. These differences in psycholinguistic development are not related to age. The two children in this study who demonstrated almost identical, low proportions of holophrastic speech, Katie, and Jordan, were respectively the youngest and oldest children included in the study.

The current study was not longitudinal, and no attempt was made to trace the change in the types of holophrases employed by a child throughout the holophrastic period, although notes were made of changes from the observation to training and follow-up portions of the study. Other theoretical writers (Werner and Kaplan, 1963) have described changes which should occur over the course of this period, and other recent investigators (Smith, 1970; Greenfield et al., 1972; Bloom, 1973; Antinucci & Parisi, 1973, Nelson, 1973) have described changes which they observed in selected children. Each of these have dealt with only one of the three aspects of language acquisition proposed here: expression of linguistic relations, cognitive understanding of relationships in the physical and social world, or an adaptation of idiosyncratic verbal productions and communicative systems to the arbitrary shared system of interactive communication in use around the child. A longitudinal study aimed at revealing changes in the relationship of these three factors for individual children as they proceed in the acquisition process will be extremely important.

Much of the work on holophrastic usage contains an implicit assumption that the holophrastic expression of relations is developmentally more advanced than any other function which single-word expression might serve (e.g. de Laguna, 1927; Greenfield, Smith, and Laufer, in press). For example, relational usage is considered to demonstrate 'more' than 'simple' naming or 'simple' imitation – if this were true, then one would expect children in this study who showed the highest proportions of holophrastic usage to show the lowest proportions of imitation and naming. The actual results show no clear relationship for the ten children as a group. In both the observation and training portions of the study, however, the child (not the same child for the two portions) with the highest proportion of repetition showed a very low proportion of holophrastic usage. This relationship, and a consequent developmental hypothesis, could be explained by the tripartite functional analysis of single-word usage. Since the three phenomena: holophrasis, naming, and imitation are associated with three sub-processes in language acquisition, one would expect each phenomenon to be proportionally greatest during the time in which that process was paramount developmentally. In other words, a cognitive partitioning of the external world is pre-requisite to the use of language, or for that matter, any symbolic process. The use of symbolic names to identify objects, actions, and events, therefore becomes crucial very early in the acquisition process. In order to produce names with which he can communicate effectively with those around him, however, the child must match, or at least approximate, the sound patterns and vocabulary items used by those around him. Repetition, one form of imitation, aids directly in this process, and should become frequent very early, perhaps even in conjunction with naming. The third aspect of language, the linguistic expression of relationships, can only reach its fullest form when the child begins to combine words. This does not occur until the child has been using single words for some time. As the emphasis in language acquisition shifts from cognitive understanding and vocabulary building to combinatorial expression, there may be an increase in the relative proportion of holophrastic usage, coupled with a decrease in naming and repetition. Since the proportion of these three at any point in development varies from child to child, such increases and decreases will only be revealed through longitudinal study.

In the longitudinal vein, it was hypothesized at the outset of this study that children showing high proportions of holophrastic speech might be closer to the point at which they began producing two-word combinations. These children would be producing more sequences of holophrases, assumed to be an intermediate step (Bloom, 1970, 1973) toward the production of true combinations, and more combinations than children with lower proportions of holophrastic speech. It has been seen in chapter 4 that this prediction was not supported. There was no connection between the proportion of holophrastic utterances, and the proportion of sequences and combinations produced. Some children with high proportions of holophrastic speech produced sequences and combinations, while others did not; a similar situation occurred for children with low proportions of holophrastic speech.

Methodological difficulties in identifying holophrases

To this point it has been assumed that this study provides evidence for the existence of holophrases, as defined here. The question of whether this definition and system of classification of holophrases is valid remains, however, and can be attacked on two grounds. First is the issue of whether the system is objective, accurate, and reliable. Second is the question of whether it is really a system at all, since it was not based on any previously defined network of known linguistic relations.

As noted many times, any system which attributes more to a child than the child actually utters must be subjective to some extent. This is especially true when extralinguistic context is involved. Someone must determine which aspects of the environment were salient to the child at a particular time; in a sense, he is attributing his own evaluation of the situation to the child. Since one cannot ask the child whether this interpretation is correct, there is essentially no way to disprove it.[1]

Every precaution was taken during this study to make this recording and classification system as accurate as possible. The notes made during experimental situations included as much of the context as possible, so that decisions could be made later as to which aspects of the environment were operating at a particular time. In several cases these notes, and background material on the tape-recordings provided the crucial information which made an utterance interpretable. Both the experimenter and the observer spent as much time as possible getting acquainted with each child and with his habitual surroundings, so that they might be aware of habitual behavioral and speech patterns. As described in chapter 3, an observer was present at training sessions. This observer devoted her entire time to recording the extralinguistic context of the utterances. All transcripts were typed by the experimenter or the observer, both of whom had been present at the sessions, so that errors in transcription would not result from the typist's lack of familiarity with the situation. Finally, all classification of utterances was done by the experimenter herself, again since she was maximally aware both of the child's speech patterns and of the extralinguistic context. The fact remains, however, that the use of this system did reveal the existence of categories which, although they varied greatly in quantity, were fairly consistent across ten children, one of the largest groups of children studied at this early stage of language acquisition to date.

Returning to the question of quantity, there is one remaining point. The

[1] An extended discussion of the point appears in chapter 1, pp. 7–8 and will not be repeated here.

psychological reality of a phenomenon, of course, does not depend upon its frequency. Piaget (1952, and elsewhere) points out that a child may have a certain capacity, and yet may display it only infrequently. In the current context, we might say that the child is able to express a particular holo-phrastic relation, yet he does not always do so. The fact that an experimenter does not observe many examples in a particular time sample, does not mean that the child cannot provide examples. Chomsky's (1957, 1965) famous competence-performance distinction comes once again to mind. There may be many variables preventing the appearance of the phenomenon at this particular time including the child's attentiveness, co-operativeness, the general appropriateness of the situation, and, of course, the child's judge-ment of appropriateness. None of these implies that the child cannot use holophrases, or even that he does not under other circumstances, but only that he will not do so at the moment, for whatever reasons. Further, a phenomenon that is infrequent, even under optimal conditions, can still be very real, and may still be important in the course of development. The discussion so far has stressed the fact that total holophrastic usage re-presents a substantial proportion of single-word speech. This fact makes it seem more likely that holophrastic usage is important in language acquisi-tion but sheer frequency is not all that matters. When one considers parti-cular holophrastic relations and the changes in frequency of some of these relations as a result of training, the numbers may be small, yet the patterns are consistent, and the relations are appropriately used by several children. While each of these changes may represent only a small part of the total pattern of psycholinguistic and cognitive abilities of a child at any one time, the changes are real, and should not be overlooked because their frequency is low.

The second objection to this system of classification is that prior to its postulation here it was not a system at all. Such a criticism does not appear to this author to be particularly relevant. Although the 'relations' described here were not all drawn from the same linguistic theories, and although some, such as 'I want', cannot be considered to be relations at all in a true linguistic sense, each one has a consistent meaning which can be identified in adult English speech, and each one has at one time or another previously been proposed to be used holophrastically by children. There is no scientific advantage in trying to fit all of the relations of any one linguistic system to children's speech rather than beginning with children's speech and identify-ing whatever relations are found, regardless of the 'system' of linguistic description from which they might be derived; this is a matter of investigative strategy. It is the contention here that since these categories permit a consistent, meaningful classification of children's single-word utterances, by that criterion they form a system.

Of course it can be argued that a particular utterance might often be described in more than one manner but this is always the case in work of this type. This system should be thought of as a working model of the way in which a child approaches the problem of language acquisition. Other systems might also describe the process; their relative utility should be judged by how useful they are in revealing regularities across children. The important point here is to discover which regularities exist, not to insist on particular names for these regularities.

The question of whether a particular utterance actually exemplifies a particular relation is more crucial. Often, the situation is similar to that described above, basically a matter of terminology. For example, one relation common in this study occurred when a child pointed to a doll, and said 'pretty'. The extralinguistic features of pointing and the presence of the doll were considered to indicate that 'pretty' referred to the doll. In this system, the relation was assumed to be '*pretty* doll', an attributive adjective modifying a noun. The utterance can equally well be interpreted, however, as 'The doll is *pretty*', an example not of an attributive, but of a predicative relation. The author believes that at this stage the difference should not matter. In either case the classification captures the fact that the child is telling something about the doll, and this is the crucial point. Since there is no basis for determining whether the child is actually considering the attributive or the predicative aspect of this communication, there is no a priori reason for preferring one classification over another. Either might have been used. In this case, the attributive was chosen because it involved the assumption of fewer words which were not expressed, but the predicative formulation might equally well have been used. Given the type of data available, one cannot assume that the child has yet distinguished between the predicative and attributive aspects; one must assume that this differentiation occurs at a later stage in acquisition. Such a distinction may indeed be semantic and not syntatic at all. It may have been a similar ambiguity which caused others to assume that predication is basic.

The same utterance can be used to illustrate another variation in classification. Suppose, for example, that the child intended to communicate, not simply '*pretty* doll', but 'This is a *pretty* doll', 'Look at the *pretty* doll', or any of an endless number of variations. This does not matter. The relation of 'pretty' to 'doll' as well as the word order remains the same in all cases;

again, why attribute more than necessary to the child? This example points out the advantage of considering holophrases to represent a consistent relation, rather than an entire sentence. Much less variability is involved in a relation than in an entire sentence; there simply is not enough evidence available, even using extralinguistic context, to determine which whole sentence the child actually intended. Similar arguments have recently been made by other authors (Greenfield, Smith, and Laufer, in press; Nelson, 1973).

The data have thus far been considered for the group as a whole because of the experimental nature of this study. The question being considered here is whether, in general, it is possible to train the two-word expression of linguistic relations. One assumes, as in all experiments, that these children are typical of normal human children at this point in their development, that in fact, their developmental histories are similar, and that for these reasons they will be similarly affected by the experimental manipulation. On the other hand, the discussion so far has also stressed the accumulated evidence (Bloom, 1970; Brown, 1973; Nelson, 1973) that language acquisition is a highly individual process which might follow a very different course in different children. The patterns of single-word utterances, sequences, and combinatorial speech obtained in this study, lend additional support to the hypothesis that language development may not be the same for all children. In a case such as this, it is most revealing to look at the changes occurring within each individual child. Grouping the data, while it allows one to identify trends, and to estimate both the strength and the generality of these trends, by its very nature obscures idiosyncratic reactions to the manipulations. It is these idiosyncratic reactions, however, which reveal functional strategy used by an individual child to discover the communication system around him. For this reason, it is important to include both a group and an individual analysis. When this was done different changes in the patterns of language from the observation to training periods were revealed for the different children. This is taken to imply that the training program affected different children in different ways. Again, the hypothesis that language acquisition is not a unitary process receives support. These changes will now be discussed in detail in the next section.

Was training of holophrastic expression of a relation into combinatorial expression of the same relation possible?

For the group of ten children as a whole, there was a significant increase in combinatorial expression of the locative and possessive relations. There was no significant increase for the subject–verb–object relation. The obvious conclusion from the group data is that in the case of the subject–verb–object relation, the training procedure did not affect the children's production either of true two-word combinations, or of sequences of holophrases which might be considered to be precursors to true combinations. In the case of the locative and possessive relations, training did appear to affect an increase. It is difficult to determine what this increase might mean, since there are no data available to determine how often the possessive and locative relations are ordinarily expressed holophrastically. Perhaps these apparently small increases are large in comparison to the total expression of these relations.

It was proposed in chapter 2 that it should be possible to train children to express in two words relations which they were already expressing holophrastically. In the case of the three relations studied here, the results are puzzling. The subject–verb–object relation was not only the only relation of the three which was expressed by all ten children during the observation period, it occurred in far greater quantity than either the locative or the possessive relation. Yet, there was no significant difference in the sequential or combinatorial expression of this relation during the training period. On the other hand, both the locative and possessive relations were expressed by only a few children and in very small quantity during observation, yet there was a significant increase in combinatorial expression of both these relations during the training period. There is, however, no association between whether or not the child was holophrastically expressing the locative or possessive relations during observation, and whether or not he combinatorially expressed these relations during training. Only one child who had been holophrastically expressing locatives during observation combinatorially expressed them during training; however, one of these had already been producing combinatorial possessives during observation. One basic assumption of this study, then, has not been supported. It appears to be possible to train some combinatorial expression, but previous holophrastic expression of the relation is certainly not pre-requisite. There was no relation between the number of training examples presented to a child and the percentage of either sequential or combinatorial expression of a relation. The only exception to this was an imperfect trend for children who received many examples of the subject–verb–object relation to express combinatorially this relation more often. With these results, one cannot explain the training as a result of quantity of example, i.e. number of opportunities provided for combinatorial expression.

It had been hoped that the successful training of only those relations which had been expressed holophrastically would demonstrate continuity between the single-word and combinatorial periods of language acquisition. It is fairly clear that such training of relations already being expressed was unsuccessful, while there was some success in training of combinatorial speech. It is by no means clear, however, that this implies discontinuity between the two periods. There are many reasonable explanations for these results. It is possible that the expression of linguistic relations is not the key which enables the child to begin to produce two-word combinations. As noted above, there not only appears to be no simple relationship between holophrastic and combinatorial expression of the same relation, there also appear to be no simple relationship between a child's total proportion of holophrastic speech and the proportion of combinatorial and sequential speech which he produces. The question of what it is that is necessary to move the child out of the single-word period, if it is not the ability to express a relation holophrastically, will be discussed in the next section.

Again, there were changes in the children's patterns of sequential and combinatorial utterances during the training period. Although the increase in combinatorial expression of locatives and possessives was small, it was statistically significant. As discussed in preceding sections, this fact does not make it any more 'real', i.e., any more valid as a construct for describing cognitive processes within the child, but it does show that the magnitude of the changes produced during the study was not as small as might have appeared at first. One interesting point is that there was also a significant increase during training in the combinatorial expression of one of the non-target relations, the negative. The negative relation had been expressed holophrastically by nine of the ten children during observation, yet, like the locative and possessive, the quantity of expression was much smaller than other relations, including the subject–verb–object and the 'I want' categories. Many of the instances of negatives, of course, may have been the result of the pressure to perform which was put upon the child by the training procedure; he said 'no'. Such an effect should not be considered trivial since it demonstrates both that the child is aware of the demands of verbal environment, and that his more usual pattern of verbal production can be readily influenced by the content and tone of this verbal environment. In addition, there were sufficient examples of other types of negatives to cause one to wonder whether the training procedure had another effect. It should be recalled that there did appear to be a general increase in patterned speech during the training period. It is quite possible that the training procedure somehow directed the children's attention to the salience of patterned speech and led to the production of more sequences and combinations, even though the numbers produced were small in comparison to total verbal output. It is also possible that while the training procedures called their attention to patterned speech, the children had not yet overcome some physiological or neurological limitation which prevented the production of many two-word combinations. This may even have produced frustration at the inability to perform, and hence the increase in negatives! This last possibility is largely speculative, of course, and will be discussed in the next section. There is also the possibility, unusual as it might sound, that training succeeded to the extent that it did with relations which the children were not expressing to a large extent precisely because it called their attention to something new. It is possible that this might be all one can expect of a training procedure aimed at processes such as cognitive development or language acquisition which are unitary and tightly interrelated in nature. It may be impossible to alter one aspect of linguistic competence without altering the entire system; it may also be virtually impossible to affect the natural rate of acquisition, yet it may be possible to initiate development in a particular area through attention-directing procedures when similar development has already begun in other areas. In this case, then, training would have had no effect on relations such as subject–verb–object which the children were already expressing in quantity, precisely because they were already aware of these, and natural acquisition processes had begun. According to this formulation, then, external training procedures serve as attention-guiding mechanisms and triggers for internal development. Still another possibility which has already been raised is that there are alternate paths which children can follow in acquiring language. For some children, training may have served a triggering function. For others, perhaps those who view language as primarily having a different function, that of the expression of linguistic relations either basically referential or social, this training procedure may simply not have been relevant.

Of course, one can always claim that this particular procedure was ill chosen or not given in sufficiently large doses and that a different procedure might have been more effective in producing combinatorial speech. Since the procedure employed here was specifically adapted to the situation, especially to fit within the children's assumed general level of over-all competence, there appears to be no basis for this claim, although the amount of training may not have been sufficient.

Finally, there are questions of experimental technique and design. As in all previous studies of single-word speech, there was no control group included in this study. Such an inclusion was desirable, but is practically impossible. In effect, by choosing children who were expressing one, but not all three target relations, each child served as his own control. The inclusion of such a group would have provided a baseline against which to judge the changes which occurred and is strongly urged in other research of this type. The data obtained from the observation portion of this research might well provide a baseline in future studies.

Another methodological issue is the accuracy of the sampling procedure, both in the design of the study as a whole, and in the data selected for analysis. Of course, one-hour and one-and-a-half-hour sessions represent only a small proportion of a child's linguistic output. This is a limitation which is inherent in all studies of this type. As much as possible, the data were supplemented by the children's mothers' reports of what happened during the remainder of the day. This information has been discussed throughout the preceding chapters. In most cases, however, the differences between what happened within and out of the experimental sessions was a question of quantity rather than variation in types of abilities displayed. In short, then, even though it is impossible to eliminate the sampling process, it does not appear to involve error of a large magnitude, assuming a large enough sample is chosen. Even the amount of data available from this sample proved massive, and it was necessary to initiate another 'sampling procedure' in selecting portions of the tape-recording to be analyzed here. This procedure is another inherent source of error. The author is aware of at least one instance in which Lia provided a beautiful example of the possessive relation. This example did not appear on the taped segment, and the data indicate that Lia provided no possessive examples. It can only be hoped that this did not occur very often; in the long run, the procedure used should have 'evened out' inequities in samples from different children. Due to this source of error, however, all known examples of relations were considered in the interpretation of the data presented here, regardless of whether they appeared numerically in the tables. With all these considerations, the author is confident that a complete analysis of all the data would not have materially altered the results obtained and discussed here.

In summary, the training procedure appears to have been effective in increasing the production of combinatorial speech for these ten children considered as a group. There was an increase in the combinatorial expression of the locative, and negative relations, and over-all there appears to have been a small increase in the total amount of patterned speech. It is possible that the training procedures served as an attention-directing mechanism and a triggering device for naturally occurring processes of language acquisition in at least some of the children. There is no evidence that holophrastic expression of a relation enhances the effectiveness of training in combinatorial expression of that relation.

If it is not holophrastic expression of linguistic relations, what is necessary to move a child into the combinatorial period?

As explained in the preceding section, it was generally possible during this study to train a child to produce small numbers of two-word combinations, regardless of whether a child was previously expressing the same relation holophrastically. The next question, then, is whether the study provided any evidence about what is necessary to cause a child to enter the combinatorial period. As mentioned above, it is assumed that the child's previous psycholinguistic development must have reached a certain point, although it is unclear just what that point is. The possibility has also been mentioned that there might be neurological or physiological limitations which must be overcome, in addition to and independent of the course of psycholinguistic and cognitive development.

The first, rather trivial possibility is that some physiological limitation prevents the child from uttering more than one word at a time. Calculations made during the course of this study have shown that during the same time period in which children produce few two-word combinations, they produce a substantially larger number of combinations of meaningful words with non-meaningful sounds. There should be no difference, of course, in the physical production of non-meaningful as opposed to meaningful sounds. The presence of these non-meaningful combinations, then, would indicate that it is not the child's inability to produce several sounds together which prevents the emergence of two-word combinations.

The three categories of non-meaningful sounds considered here did not seem to have much theoretical implication. The 'mm sound' was separated because it was first believed that this sound would appear largely in connection with foods and eating; this notion was quickly dismissed. The schwa sound has been suggested (Bloom, 1973) as a precursor to true combination, since it appeared to serve as a 'placeholder' in combination with other words for one child. The current study, however, indicates that the schwa sound appears in combination with words no more frequently than the 'other sounds' taken together. It is possible that any sound could serve as a placeholder, but this study provides no evidence either for or against this possibility. There is, however, some evidence that most of these combinations should not be considered relational. With the exception of combinations of 'mm' plus a word, there is a tendency for all other combinations, including those with the schwa sound, to appear in inverted order, i.e. word followed by sound as well as the more usual word preceded by sound. As mentioned in chapters 1 and 2, the invariability of word order has been used by many previous investigators (see Brown, 1973; McNeill, 1970b; Bloom, 1970) as one good indicator that a combination is relational. It is of interest that, in contrast, it was found in this study that both true two-word combinations and to a lesser extent sequences of holophrases rarely appear in inverted word order, at least one indication that these are truly relational in nature. In this study, sequences were intermediate in variability between combinations with non-meaningful sounds and true two-word combinations. This contrasts somewhat with Bloom's (1973) finding that sequences are variable in word order. The case of non-meaningful combinations with 'mm' is unusual. It is possible, of course, that these combinations are relational, and that 'mm' really is not a 'non-meaningful sound' for the child but actually has word status. This intriguing suggestion might well be followed up by further research.

Some investigators (Bloom, 1970, 1973; Greenfield et al., in press; Smith, 1970) have suggested that the appearance of sequences of holophrases is a good indication that the appearance of combinatorial speech is soon to follow. Again, the present study was not longitudinal in nature, so it is not possible to speak directly to this issue. The training procedure, however, had no significant effect on the number of sequences which the children produced.

One might think that a sequence, aside from the pause involved, is essentially no different from a combination, and that perhaps the two categories should be collapsed, thereby increasing the proportion of the children's speech which could be considered to be combinatorial. McNeill has done some preliminary analysis of data from this study (McNeill, 1974). These results indicate not only that there are noticeable differences in the length of the pause between words in sequences and combinations, as was self-evident from the classification procedure, but also that there are observably different patterns in intonation contours. This preliminary evidence at least would indicate that sequences of holophrases do not yet share the properties of combinatorial speech, and should not be considered as such.

All the above considerations deal with factors which for various reasons could not be responsible for the emergence of combinatorial speech. The question still remains as to what is responsible. Some well-guided speculation is perhaps in order. First, one can still insist that some pre-requisite amount of psycholinguistic development is necessary before combinatorial speech can appear, even though there is no indication of what this development entails.

One possible implication of this study is the elimination of the most obvious psycholinguistic pre-requisites, i.e. the ability to use language relationally, the ability to produce more than one sound at a time, and the ability to produce at least some sequences or combinations in constant word order. Since no other psycholinguistic abilities come immediately to mind as necessary precursors to combinatorial speech, it is possible that all the conditions have been met on the psycholinguistic side, and that the crucial variable is not psycholinguistic at all, but neurological or physiological.

There are an almost infinite number of possibilities which might be investigated, e.g. memory, or perhaps even brain size or amount of brain tissue available. McNeill (1972) has made one intriguing suggestion. Perhaps the crucial variable is some mechanism for imposing serial order on a string of words; such a mechanism was proposed long ago by Lashley (1951). Since combinatorial speech, once it has begun to develop soon involves large numbers of words which must appear in certain patterns of order fixed by the grammar of the language, such an assumption seems highly plausible. The children in this study were producing some sequences and combinations in fixed order, but their number was extremely small. In the entire study, there was only one example of a three-word combination, when Ricky looked in an empty purse and exclaimed, 'no more money!' It is possible that although a few two-word combinations had just begun to appear, these children could not begin to produce combinatorial speech freely and in large quantity until some mechanism for imposing serial order on more than two words had developed. The possibility remains open.

In summary, this study provides evidence that certain factors probably are not responsible for the onset of combinatorial speech. These include the relational use of holophrases, the appearance of combinations of non-meaningful words, and the fixed order which occurs in the few sequences and combinations which do appear. There is no evidence for other possible psycholinguistic factors which might trigger the onset of combinatorial speech. In speculation, it was suggested that some independent factor might be responsible, particularly some mechanism for imposing serial order on a string of words (Lashley, 1951) as has been proposed by McNeill.

What information does this study provide about the relation of language development during the single-word period to cognitive, or sensory-motor development?

As has already been mentioned, the information about sensory-motor abilities obtained during this study is incomplete. Much further research is necessary in order to get a clear picture, both of the true pattern of the children's sensory-motor abilities, and of the relationship between these abilities and psycholinguistic abilities. This is partly due to the fact that it is unclear just how much sensory-motor development must precede the beginning of representational abilities, and partly due to methodological difficulties within the study itself. Because there has been so little experimental work with children of this age, tests of the core skills of symbolic play and deferred imitation were devised specifically for the study. Some of the advantages of and difficulties with the process will be described below. The proposed cognitive correlate abilities to linguistic relations were tested, and do not appear truly to be correlate abilities. With both groups of tests, the core skills and the proposed correlates, it was extremely difficult to secure the children's attention and co-operation. For this reason, it is unclear whether these results reflect their maximum capabilities.

One difficulty with the tests of deferred imitation, symbolic play, and role playing was their dependence upon verbal instructions. In several cases, the children simply were not interested in attempting the tasks, perhaps because they could not understand the instructions. In some instances, the children were willing to try but simply could not perform; it was the experimenter's subjective impression that they did not understand what was expected of them. It is suggested here that in any further experimental investigation of these skills, the tests depend as much as possible on non-verbal instructions. Even with these precautions, it may be difficult to design ideal tests. In his discussion of these abilities, Piaget (1952, and elsewhere) deals largely with their spontaneous expression. Indeed, the element of spontaneity may be crucial in this case in determining whether a child truly has an internalized ability or whether he is merely mimicking an experimenter's demonstration. Spontaneous demonstrations of all these skills were recorded during the course of this study, but they by no means provided a complete picture of the children's abilities in these areas. It was hoped that the inclusion in this study of standardized sensory-motor tasks would provide comparable data for several children, and would free experimenters from hours of waiting for an appropriate skill to be displayed spontaneously. It was also hoped that a comprehensive battery would provide a more complete picture of each child's sensory-motor skills than could be obtained by naturalistic methods in so short a period of time. The idea still seems sound, but future experimenters should be cautioned regarding both the difficulty in capturing that elusive element of spontaneity in a structured task and also the practical problems of maintaining interest, co-operation and attention.

Sensory-motor correlates to the psycholinguistic relations

In the case of the possessive relation, it was considered so difficult to establish a cognitive correlate with no verbal content that one was not included in the study. The correlate pair which seemed most intuitively obvious was the displacement series correlate to the locative relation; it seemed to follow that the correlate to the ability to say where an object was is the ability actively to find it. Even in this case, however, it is not clear how much of the displacement series must be successfully completed. Although Piaget claims that most children can retrieve an object after two invisible displacements by the close of the sensory-motor period, it would seem that retrieval after only a single visible displacement would be basis enough for the cognitive correlate, since the notion of object and a specific location are both included. The entire series was included in the study to provide additional information about the children's abilities. It has already been shown that if one considers the results of the entire series, there is no relation between success on the cognitive task and holophrastic expression of locatives. Even if one looks only at the single visible displacement, the results remain unclear. Four children expressed locatives holophrastically, and eight succeeded at the single visible displacement task. Of the four children who used holophrastic locatives, however, one did not succeed at the sensory-motor task, and in one case the sensory-motor task was not administered. The evidence, then, seems neither to support nor disprove the contention that the two abilities are true correlates; there simply are not enough data available to tell.

In the case of both proposed correlates to the subject–verb–object relation, there is much less confusion. The results do not support the contention that either task is a correlate to the holophrastic ability; there is no obvious pattern of relation for either task. Some children who did well on one task or the other used a high proportion of holophrastic subject–verb–object expression, and some did not; the same was true for those children who showed lower proportions of holophrastic expression. In the case of the two-part task involving the ability to use one object to act upon another, and then to reverse this, there was no apparent relation to either the forward, or the reverse ability.

Similarly, there was no obvious relation between level of performance on the stacking-cups task, and holophrastic expression of subject–verb–object. The pattern of results on the task itself was similar to that obtained by Greenfield et al. (1972). They found that the simplest, or pairing strategy was dominant at eleven months of age, forms intermediate between pairing and pots were dominant at sixteen months, pots became dominant at twenty months, and sub-assemblies later still. Greenfield et al. claimed that the ability to put one cup down and pick up another cup to use in another action is one indication of an actor–object differentiation. Further refinements in this ability, as represented by the more complicated strategies, are claimed to be analogous to compound subjects and embedded sentences. This study seems to substantiate the findings, but not the interpretation. Children in this study ranged in age from sixteen to twenty-two months, being mostly sixteen and seventeen months' old, and they were intermediate in dominance between the pairing and pot strategies. Since they all produced at least pairs, they can all be assumed, according to Greenfield et al. to have differentiated between actors and objects. As explained in detail in chapter 1, however, it is not the differentiation between actor, or subject and object, but the relationship between them once they have been differentiated which is crucial to linguistic ability, so that this finding has little bearing on the question involved. Further, there was no relationship between the children's differing levels of ability on this task and their proportion of holophrastic expression of the subject–verb–object relation. It is possible that performance on this task depends largely upon the development of the abilities involved in seriation or perhaps with inclusion relations and double functioning on the sensory-motor level rather than on language acquisition. Since the agent–action–object relation to which Greenfield et al. refer is only one of the semantic manifestations of the syntactic relation subject–verb–object included in this study, it is suggested that further studies consider only agent–action–object relations. In any case, none of the three tasks proposed in this study as cognitive correlates to psycholinguistic abilities was firmly established as such.

The more general question, of whether it is fruitful, or even reasonable to search for cognitive correlates to linguistic relations remains. The results of this study rule out only the specific tasks chosen. Yet these tasks seemed the most obvious. The difficulty which adults have in finding such tasks may testify to the fact that they are 'correlates' constructed by adults and without any psychological reality for the children who are supposed to be acquiring the ability to understand them. The cognitive correlates were originally thought of as pre-requisite, action-bound capacities which the child must possess before he can acquire parallel capacities on a symbolic level. The results of this study indicate that at least for the tasks tested, there is no evidence for such a one-to-one correspondence between sensory-motor and symbolic abilities. It is perhaps more promising to search for basic sensory-motor abilities as pre-requisite to language, i.e. to search for building blocks rather than templates.

The first methodological question, whether a true picture of the children's abilities on these tasks was obtained, remains open. All one can say is that even with the precautions taken in designing and administering the tasks to maximize interest and co-operation, the children's response was far from optimal. A certain amount of difficulty can always be expected in maintaining the attention and securing the co-operation of such young children. It is hoped, however, that other investigators will continue to try to devise tasks which can be used to supplement the data obtained from naturalistic observations and which will provide a standardized, objective, and comprehensive picture of the sensory-motor skills of single-word speakers.

Core sensory-motor skills

With all the limitations which ensued, considerable information was nevertheless obtained about the over-all pattern of sensory-motor abilities for each child. The patterns were often very different across the group, so that it is difficult to make general statements. It is clear, however, that every child succeeded on at least one of the three basic representational abilities: symbolic play, deferred imitation, and role playing. Most children showed some examples of all but role playing. Only one child, Jessica, showed evidence of role playing ability. This, of course, does not imply that the other nine children have not completed sensory-motor development, since this skill only has its roots during this period, and matures later. The test was included because role playing is one aspect of the symbolic function, as described by Piaget. Part of the object of this study was to determine whether or not the children displayed other symbolic skills at about the same time that the process of language acquisition began. A total of eight children succeeded at symbolic play, and eight at deferred imitation. Further, there were only two instances among all the tests of these three skills on which a child actually failed; in all other cases he refused to co-operate.

The appearance of these two basic abilities, symbolic play and deferred imitation, considered in light of the pattern presented by the individual children, indicates that in general the children included in this study appear to have completed, or at least almost completed, the period of sensory-motor development as described by Piaget. Accepting the contention that role playing is not really a sensory-motor skill, one must conclude, as Piaget did, that at least in temporal sequence the completion of the sensory-motor period precedes the appearance of combinatorial speech. Sinclair-de-Zwart (1969) stresses 'simultaneity of onset' as one characteristic of the symbolic function. This symbolic function, of course, includes deferred imitation, symbolic play, role playing, and combinatorial speech. A short time-delay between the appearance of deferred imitation and symbolic play as compared to role playing and combinatorial speech would not seriously affect the claim of simultaneity of onset.

The data indicate one possible discrepancy with the work of Piaget and his followers. They claim that the ability to retrieve an object which has undergone two invisible displacements appears at about the end of the sensory-motor period. Of the eight children in this study to whom the series was administered, all succeeded after a single visible displacement, five after two invisible displacements, two after one invisible displacement, and one after two invisible displacements. Again, there were only four actual failures among many refusals to co-operate. It is, of course, possible that the children's performance on this task was not truly reflecting their ability. This performance alone, although it is contrary to expectation, is not sufficient evidence to claim that the children have not completed sensory-motor development. Yet it does raise questions. Why do these children not demonstrate the ability to retrieve an object after two visible displacements, as Piaget claims they should? Perhaps the failure was due to the design or the administration of the task, although it is still peculiar that this particular task, on which it had been expected that almost all the children would succeed, should provide the impetus for a widespread refusal to perform. If one accepts the notion that these children using single-word speech are indeed functioning on a symbolic level, then this study could be interpreted as indicating that the ability to retrieve an object after two invisible displacements is not pre-requisite to the symbolic use of language. As for the question of whether these children have completed sensory-motor developments, this may be an example of décalage, i.e. a time lag or discrepancy in the appearance of functions which depend on the same underlying cognitive abilities.

The ability to retrieve after a succession of invisible displacements is important in Piaget's theory, since it indicates the child's awareness of object permanence. Object permanence, in turn, is a pre-requisite for the appearance of the symbolic function. Given these children's performance on the tests of symbolic play and deferred imitation, together with their psycholinguistic ability, they appear to be operating at least some of the time on a symbolic level. If one accepts the performance on the displacement task as reflecting the children's true ability, and, if the time lag in appearance of this ability is determined from longitudinal studies to be great, then one must say either that the children are not truly symbolic, or that this ability to retrieve after a succession of displacements is not pre-requisite to the development of symbolic function. The latter explanation seems more reasonable here, especially since all eight children tested succeeded at the minimum requirement of retrieval after one visible displacement. This may be all the object permanence necessary for the appearance of symbolic function, including an early language in which words readily shift phonological form, in which words take on new referents, and become both more and less generic, and in which the two elements of a relation may be alternately expressed. Single-word children, including those in this study, are taking a first stab, as it were, at the communication system which functions in the world around them, but at this time neither that system nor the world and the objects in it appear to be very permanent.

One must conclude, then, that with the exception of one major ability, retrieval of an object after a series of invisible displacements, these children have basically completed sensory-motor development, while they have not yet entered the period of combinatorial speech. Excluding this question of object permanence, there is not other evidence to dispute Sinclair-de-Zwart's claim that completion of sensory-motor development is necessary, although not sufficient, for the development of representational intelligence in the form of combinatorial speech. This does not imply, however, that children cannot use language relationally before the appearance of combinatorial speech. On the contrary, the study has provided evidence for the holophrastic use of single-words as a major phenomenon during this period. This relational use does not conflict with Piaget's and Sinclair-de-Zwart's position but is a refinement of this position. It involves representational abilities, and it appears at about the same time as or even slightly before other representational abilities, such as symbolic play and deferred imitation. The results with respect to object permanence are surprising and should be investigated further. As for the proposed cognitive correlates to linguistic relations, the two suggested correlates to the subject–verb–object relation (the ability to use one object to act upon another, and the stacking-cups task) appear to have little actual relation to the linguistic ability. No clear relation is apparent for the displacement series as a possible correlate to the locative relation.

The question of form-preference

There is one segment of the data which has not been discussed thus far because it does not bear directly upon any of the four preceding questions. This is the results of the test for form-preference. This test was included for methodological reasons, as a guide to determining the type of utterance which would be most appropriate for the training procedure. Since the children in this study showed little preference in the type of command obeyed, both child-form or incomplete utterances, and complete utterances were used during the training period.

Unlike the children in the Shipley et al. (1969) study, these children responded to few of the commands given. This may in part be due to methodological differences in administration, and in part to the practice here of scoring only those instances in which the child performed an action with an object, as opposed to the Shipley et al. practice of scoring all glances and approaches toward an object, and the Nelson (1973) method of giving partial credit for such glances and approaches. Among the small number of commands obeyed, few children in this study showed a preference in the types of commands obeyed. Children in this study were in the youngest age range of children studied by Shipley et al. Further, when the absolute length of each command is considered, in relation to the number of long and short commands administered, there is also no marked preference demonstrated. These results are similar to those obtained by Nelson (1973) and might imply that the length of the utterances used by adults in addressing children who are just acquiring language will not materially affect the children's comprehension as measured by their ability to respond correctly. It is rather discouraging, in this study at least, that ability to respond was very poor under both experimental conditions. As has been recently remarked by Nelson (1973), the relation of adult and of child comprehension to other indices of language acquistion must be another important area of investigation.

*In summary, how should one characterize the single-word period of
language acquisition? What is the relationship between the single-word
period and later language acquisition?*

The data obtained from this study are rich, and their implications are broad,
touching upon both the structure and function of single-word speech, the
relation between single-word and combinatorial speech, and the relation
between language acquisition and other preceding and concurrent processes
of cognitive development. The study is not longitudinal, so that it is impossible from these data to trace the development in any or all of these spheres
during the single-word period, yet the theoretical ramifications are many,
and the suggestions for further research cannot be overlooked. What follows
is not meant to be a complete theory of single-word speech, but rather a set
of experimentally based hypotheses to guide and direct future efforts.

The first point is that there are major differences in the acquisition
patterns for these ten children. Although all ten were chosen because they
seemed to be at approximately the same level of language development, i.e.
they all had been using single words for several months, there were great
variations, which have been already discussed in detail, in the way in which
each child used single words. The proportions of the child's speech which
could be classified as holophrastic, naming, and repetition or imitation of
adult speech varied a great deal.

It has been suggested earlier that the three phenomena – holophrasis,
naming, and repetition, reflect three different processes in language acquisition: respectively, the child's preliminary awareness of linguistic relations
and structure in adult speech, the classification of objects in the surround-
ing world, and the matching of sound patterns and vocabulary items to the
models provided in the community. Repetition might also involve the child's
awareness of the communication dyad, a first attempt to direct his talking
to another person. In this approach, the differing proportions of these three
types of single-word utterances in different children's speech might reflect
differing functional approaches to the problem of language acquisition.

Nelson (1973) has proposed two functional groups of children she calls
referential and expressive. The distinction is based upon a vocabulary
analysis. Referential children know and use a large number of object-words
while expressive children use predominantly other kinds of words. There
are some differences in acquisition patterns for these two groups of children
over the ten to twenty-five month period. Nelson claims that referential
children are oriented toward interpreting and classifying the world around

them, using language as a tool for doing this, while expressive children are more interpersonally oriented, and view language primarily as a system of communication between people.

The results of this study have independently led to a similar possible division of early language users according to their functional approach to the language-learning problem. A large proportion of holophrastic speech may indicate an orientation toward discovering the key to the language used by others, i.e. an interest in syntactic and semantic structure. A large proportion of naming may reflect a child's concern with the classification and categorization of the world around him. A large proportion of repetition may reveal a concern with the interpersonal and communicative aspects of language, both the two-party or sender and receiver nature of the system, as well as the importance of sending the correct, culturally defined signals, i.e. words.

Of course, one must not forget that while the proportions of these three processes varied from child to child, all three were operating in each child, and in substantial quantity. To date, with the exception of Nelson (1973) and Brown (1973) most studies of early language have focused on one or the other of these aspects, to the exclusion of the other. Studies of syntax (Bellugi and Brown, 1964; Braine, 1963; McNeill, 1966) have by and large not dealt with the issue of language as a system of communication. Studies of the effect of cognitive development on early utterances (Bloom, 1973) have played down the child's awareness of syntactic structure, and so on. One important conclusion of this study is that these three interdependent processes are operating concurrently. If one is truly to understand the beginnings of language acquisition, then one must study the child's changing cognitive skill in classifying and understanding the world around him, his progress in communicating effectively with others, and his awareness of both syntactic and semantic relations. Each child's progress in language acquisition at the single-word stage appears to be some unique interplay among these three factors. Since all three are important, from the child's point of view, the adult excluding any one of these in his studies will find his understanding of the child's language necessarily incomplete.

The relationship between these three processes involved in language acquisition, and the three mechanisms which reflect their operation in single-word speech is shown in the figure on page 119. One can conceptualize the situation by imagining that the child who does not yet use the shared language system is faced with the problem of discovering the fact that such a system exists, finding out how it operates, and then learning to use it himself. The problem is divided into several sub-problems because language itself is not a unitary ability. First, language is a symbolic system, one in which entities from the language – sound, words, and combinations of words, represent other entities outside the language – objects, actions, and events and the relations between these. In order to utilize such a symbol system, the child must first understand that there are objects, actions, and events in the world which exist separate from himself and he must understand that symbols, elements of language can represent objects, actions, and relationships which are not present. This, of course, is the cognitive base prerequisite for the emergence of language, as has been discussed in detail by Piaget and by others. It is easy to understand how naming, the process repeatedly demonstrated to comprise such a large proportion of single-word speech (de Laguna, 1927; Werner and Kaplan, 1963; Brown, 1958; Greenfield, Smith, and Laufer, in press), could serve the function of establishing relationships between symbols, entities within the language system, and the objects, events, actions, and relationships in the external world which can be depicted through the use of language.

Yet language is more than a representational system or symbolic process, it is a system of communication by which one person can make his internal states public. The child must become aware very early that the others around him are using such a system, and that this enables them to do things for one another which he cannot do efficiently through such diffuse, non-specific mechanisms as crying. From the child's point of view, this aspect of the problem is twofold. He must discover the shared symbols which are in use around him, and learn to produce those, and he must learn the rules of conversational give and take that allow one person to send a message, receive a response, and in turn respond appropriately. At first, overt repetition serves both these purposes. It enables the child to match the verbal symbols being produced by others around him, and to respond to another's verbal input with a verbal message of his own. Of course, this is not a very efficient means of communication, since it generally adds nothing new to the conversation, and it may be an inappropriate response to the demand or request being made of the child. Eventually, other modalities including appropriate responding to questions, questioning, and demanding by the child, must be added to his communicative repertoire.

Still, there is more to the complicated system of language than even the symbolic and communicative aspect combined. Each known human language is governed by a syntactic and semantic combinatorial system which cannot be explained as the direct outgrowth of prior cognitive development and which cannot be acquired through imitation. Somehow, children discover the rules of combination which govern a particular language. It is the expression of these linguistic relationships, both syntactic and semantic, which begins during the single-word period as holophrasis, the expression of a linguistic relation through the use of a single word.

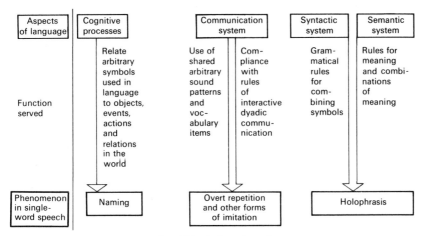

A model for single-word speech

Such a tripartite conceptualization easily permits the developmental hypothesis put forward earlier in this chapter, that for an individual child, the proportion of his single-word speech devoted to each of these processes will change as the symbolic process, the communicative process, and the rules of linguistic combination, become the problem of developmental import. Although no evidence is found in a cross-sectional study such as this one, there is some supporting data from the other sources reviewed in chapter 1. De Laguna (1927), Werner and Kaplan (1963) and Greenfield, Smith, and Laufer (in press) report that naming predominates early in the use of single words, and is later joined and perhaps superceded by such processes as predication. Some evidence on the question of imitation is provided by Nelson (1973) who claims that large amounts of imitation are indicative of advanced linguistic development at twenty-one months, and retarded development at twenty-four months. Rodgon and Kurdek (1975) report that elicited vocal imitation is positively correlated with an estimate of vocabulary at fourteen and twenty months, but not correlated with a mean length of utterance measure at twenty months.

Further, this tripartite scheme would neatly explain the functional differences between children who focus on different aspects of the language problem during acquisition. The tremendous individual differences between acquisition patterns presented by different children would be much more understandable, if one recognized that there is indeed more than one kind of acquisition occurring, and that the existence of optional functional strategies does not mean that 'syntactic', 'semantic', 'cognitive', or 'communicative' explanations must be rejected outright.

Indeed, until very recently these four kinds of explanations – syntactic, semantic, cognitive, and communicative, have been viewed as alternatives, one of which must correctly represent the process of language acquisition to the exclusion of all others. After the introduction of transformational grammar (Chomsky 1957, 1965) with the revelation that grammar could not be learned either through direct reinforcement or direct imitation, the emphasis in language acquisition studies was on the acquisition of syntax (McNeill, 1966; Bellugi and Brown, 1964; Ervin-Tripp, 1964; Braine, 1963; to name a few). It soon became apparent that there was more to language than grammar, and that the remarkable commonalities which were first noticed among children acquiring different languages gave way to several alternate patterns of acquisition as more and more children were studied. Bloom (1970) led the way in incorporating semantic rules into the acquisition explanations. As the shift in linguistics turned from pure syntax to semantics (McCawley, 1968), the emphasis on semantics during acquisition became stronger and stronger. At the same time, Piagetians (Sinclair-de-Zwart, 1969) were claiming that their cognitive explanations were an alternative to the peculiarly linguistic rule systems proposed by American psycholinguists. They claimed instead, that the use of symbolic language was a necessary and logical outgrowth of prior sensory-motor development, and could be understood as another manifestation of the universal processes of cognitive development. Soon psycholinguists (McNeill, 1970; Brown, 1973) began incorporating cognitive explanations into their descriptions of language acquisition. Here, particular attention was paid to the single-word period. Both Bloom (1970, 1973) and Brown (1973) claimed that true linguistic development does not appear until the emergence of combinatorial speech, and that development before that point should be called cognitive. In their view, development during the single-word period is different in nature from the rest of the language acquisition process that follows. McNeill (1974) in a recent paper did not speak of the difference between cognitive rules and linguistic rules, but of entities he calles 'syntagmas', meaning-units which express linguistic content, and which are the direct product of previous cognitive development. Finally, Dore (1973) conducted an analysis of single-word speech in which he focuses on pragmatics, the child's awareness of the function of language as a communicative system, and he proposes this as an alternative to understanding single-word speech in terms of holophrases or linguistic relations. Nelson (1973) too speaks of understanding semantics and rules of communication during the single-word period instead of linguistic relations.

It is very clear, then, that in the years since 1971 when this study was first conceptualized, there has been a tremendous change in climate among developmental psycholinguists, and in attitudes toward single-word speech. The fact that the emergence of language is directly linked to previous cognitive development on the sensory-motor level is no longer seriously disputed, although to this author's knowledge there have been no other studies comparing abilities in the two spheres. With the focus now on semantics, cognitive pre-requisites for language, and pragmatics, interest in explaining the acquisition of syntax seems to have waned. As has been stressed repeatedly, each of the recent studies focuses on only one of these aspects. Yet, as has been argued here, it is clear that all of the essential aspects of language must be mastered if the child is to use the adult language correctly and efficiently, and therefore that any complete theory of language acquisition must explain how this mastery evolves in all four areas. The evidence from this study indicates that mechanisms relating to all of these – syntax, semantics, pragmatics, and cognitive processes, are operating to some extent during the single-word period. Of course, any utterance can be conceptualized as serving more than one function; the tripartite divisions are not *independent* in any true sense because the functional aspects of language overlap. For example, while holophrasis is the expression of both semantic and syntactic relations, the child who uses an appropriate adult word holophrastically has also both matched the adult symbolic system, and indicated a relationship between a linguistic symbol and the external world. Similarly, a process such as naming involves the development of the semantic system at the same time as the child may be primarily concerned with establishing language system–external word relationships. These interdependencies, rather than invalidating the model, once again highlight the futility of trying to consider one or more of the functional processes to the exclusion of the others.

In providing evidence for the holophrastic expression of relations in single-word speech, along with the concurrent use of naming and repetition, this study has not only served as a base for a theory of language acquisition which encompasses all the aspects of language, it has also provided preliminary answers to several questions about the legitimacy of classification as a whole, the use of extralinguistic context in classifying utterances, the relationship of language and other cognitive processes, and continuity between single-word and combinatorial speech. This study, taken with others (de Laguna, 1927; Werner and Kaplan, 1963; Smith, 1970; Greenfield, Smith, and Laufer, in press), provides substantial evidence for the relational use of single words. Clearly, the child can utter the same word in different contexts and thereby convey different meanings, just as he can utter different words in similar contexts and thereby convey similar meanings. It has been argued in chapter 1 that holophrastic utterances are best considered as conveying linguistic relations rather than entire sentences. The question of which relations are intended still has not been definitively answered. The relations chosen in this study were intended to reveal patterns of usage across these ten children, if such patterns existed, and hopefully to be available to other investigators for use in tracing longitudinal changes during the single-word period. Certainly, some uniformity in the treatment of single-word speech is needed.

The system used was successful in revealing regularities, but as a system, it is far from perfect. Other systems of relations could be used to analyze the same data or similar data. The system of modified case relations proposed by Greenfield et al. (in press) is one good candidate. One must remember that a system of linguistic relations is a description of linguistic output. Of course, there can be alternate, and often equally correct descriptions of the same output. To insist otherwise, and to claim that the child's interpretation or his generating process for the utterance is the same as the adult's would be to 'adultomorphize' the child, and would be a grave error. One implication of this study is that future systems should take account of the context of communication. Such factors as whether the child is speaking to anyone, and whether he is performing an action as he talks have been included in a new system. It is as important to discover regularities in the relationship of language to cognitive abilities on the action level and in developing dyadic communication skills as in the expression of linguistic relations.

In this regard, some final comments about context for classification purposes in this and other studies are in order. Apparently, such use is not only justified, but essential. Taking account of the concurrent situation while the child talks, particularly his own gestures and other actions, reveals regularities which would otherwise remain hidden. The results of this study suggest once again that from the child's point of view, early language is closely tied to action and therefore it cannot be fully understood by an adult if this action is not included in the analysis. Similarly, developing communication skills cannot be fully understood if the observer is unaware of whether the child initiates a conversation or replies to another person, whether that reply is appropriate to the situation, and so on. In fact, it is suggested that future researchers utilize videotaped observation whenever possible, in order to obtain complete and accurate records of context. Returning to the three-part characterization of language introduced earlier, one cannot forget that language is basically a system of communication, and that some part of every child's strategy in acquiring language must be oriented toward 'hooking in' to that system and communicating some information of his own. If one next considers what it is that the child has to communicate, this appears to consist of two parts, immediate wants and desires to which the child would like an adult to attend, and the information which he has gathered about the world. The first category is clearly action-oriented, and if one remembers that up until this time the child has gathered information almost entirely through his own actions and/or direct observation of the actions of others, then so is the second. Again, the interdependence of early language with action is illustrated.

This raises the question of the relation between language acquisition and cognitive development which has been discussed in detail in the preceding section. In addition, the following points should be noted. If so much of early language is tied to the child's action and his descriptions of the world around him, then his cognitive development, in terms of developing repertoires of action-patterns, classificatory categories for the objects around him, and rules relating these objects to one another, must clearly precede to a considerable extent the child's use of relational language, and equally clearly the child's changing cognitive organization is inextricably intertwined with his changing linguistic skills. Cognitive re-organizations must affect the communication system, just as the advent of the communication system reciprocally influences cognitive re-organization. Although it is clear that language is a symbolic system, and that a considerable amount of cognitive development precedes the ability to use symbols, this study raises some questions about how well-established symbols must be when they first appear, particularly with reference to the question of object permanence. Perhaps the child who begins to use language has an imperfect notion of object permanence, and perhaps his use of symbols fluctuates accordingly. There is no doubt, however, that on the whole, the single-word speaker has completed sensory-motor development and is displaying most of the skills which according to Piaget (Sinclair-de-Zwart, 1969) comprise the symbolic function.

Finally, this study sheds light on the issue of continuity between single-word and combinatorial speech. The three-part categorization helps highlight this continuity. First, consider naming. One can assume that the child continues from birth onward to re-organize and re-classify his world, although the form of this classification probably changes dramatically when the child becomes symbolic at the onset of the first language, and again when he becomes verbally fluent. One might hypothesize that as the child's speech becomes combinatorial, although he continues to increase his vocabulary rapidly by adding new words, or names for things, he may shift in focus from names of individual objects and events to combining and co-ordinating information he has acquired about these objects and events. This is evidenced of course by the appearance of adjectives and adverbs which add information, and conjunctions to link separate pieces of information. The process of identifying correspondences between language symbols and real-world events which was begun with single-word naming continues, although the primary emphasis is now on other aspects of language.

A second important factor in language acquisition, the child's focus on the communicative dyad, is evidenced by the child's use of repetition. As noted, this is only a beginning, and repetition is not the most effective means of communicating new information. One would expect that as the child becomes fluent in language, he would rely less or repetition and increasingly on setting-up situations which require a response, i.e. questions or commands, and in turn on responding to questions and commands directed to him. There is evidence in this study that even at the single-word stage, the child responds appropriately to questions. This is evidence both of his awareness of the linguistic relations involved in the question, and of the communicative demand for a response. Further research to identify longitudinal changes in patterns of repetition, the asking of questions, and commands and the responses to these will certainly be intriguing.

Last, evidence for continuity comes from the relational, or holophrastic aspect of single-word speech. The very fact that the same type of linguistic relations can be used to describe single-word and combinatorial speech has been discussed in detail as evidence for continuity. The phenomenon of sequences lends additional support. Sequences of single-word utterances are not truly combinatorial. This is evident from the pauses involved, and the differences in intonation contours. Yet the meaning of these somewhat separate single-word utterances is interpretable as combinatorial speech. They seem to be a transition between the two types of language usage, sharing properties of both. Further, they do not ordinarily appear in inverted order. This should be accepted as evidence for their grammaticality by those who are reluctant to grant this status to single-word utterances (Bloom, 1973; Brown, 1973). In light of all these facts, it does not seem logical to consider the single-word period to be different in nature from combinatorial speech, or that these two periods are separated by some barrier involving the discovery of linguistic relations.

The preceding hypotheses sketch an outline for the understanding of this important period in language acquisition and cognitive development. What happens during this time lays important groundwork for all that follows, yet it too has been prepared for. Other investigators have painstakingly laid the groundwork in the investigation of single-word speech. It is the author's hope that this admittedly preliminary study, together with the many hypotheses which now must be proven, will help provide a foundation for fruitful investigations yet to come.

Appendix A Sample transcripts: observation sessions

DEANNA

2nd observation, age 19 months 12 days (uncle Sonny present)

E: Here's your box (E hands her tape box)	open
E: Is that the right side, huh? (E opens and shuts it twice; D takes it, then comes to E with box)	opun (she is asking E to open it)
	open
E: (opening it) How come you keep closing it up if you want it opened?	open
E: (laughing) I think we got a game going here.	
Sonny: Yeah.	boonuh
(E asks Sonny for clarification)	
	uh
	(t.r. makes noise, E explains)
	(back with box)
	open
	wuh pen
S: (holding clown) Who's this, Deanna?	huh
S: Who is that? Who is that? Who is it?	clown
S: Bozo.	beewo

E: Deanna. Look.	mmooee
E: Hey, silly.	nah (D runs out of room to S)
S: (coaxing her back)	
	(walks over to t.r., looking at top)
	open
E: (laughs)	uh opun (accent on second syllable)
E: What will you do if I open it, huh?	
	buh bukah
E: (opens it) Don't touch. Don't touch. Just look.	
E: Pretty?	

E: What is that? Can you say tape?
   Tape.   (touches t.r. case)
                                     nice

E: nice? Is it nice? (E picks up mike,
   holds out to D) Say hi! Hi!   (D listens, instead of talking)
E: It doesn't make any noise.
S: (unintelligible)
E: It doesn't make any noise. (just then
   it starts making noises)
   That's a funny noise, huh?   huh
E: (unintelligible)   noise
E: Noise.   (she touches back of t.r. case)
                                       noise

E: Aren't you a good girl? Are you a
   good girl?   no
E: No? Are you a bad girl, huh?   (playing with keys)
                                       keys
                                       (long pause)
                                       Bobo!
                                       uh uh (soft)
S: No.   pabo!
S: No.   pabo
                                       taa
                                       (t.r. makes noise; D touches it)
                                       noise (but could be nice)
S: Uh uh. Don't. No. Don't bother it.
E: (closing up key case) Okay, okay.   nice (touching it again, clear)
                                       uh uh
E: Where'd it go?   open!
E: Open.   (t.r. makes noise, again, touches)
                                       nice (?)
                                       (Keys drop, she bends to pick up)
                                       Keys
                                       (closes key case)
                                       open!
                                     (cont. with keys)

Deferred imitation

E: Hey, Deanna   huh
E: Can you do this? (claps)   huh
E: Can you do that?
S: Hey (he claps)   huh
E: (claps) You do it. (she won't)
   Can you do this? (hits couch)   oh (she does it)

Good. Okay, can you do it later,
too? Later when I say can you do
it again, can you do it?

    huh
    (she hits couch again) nice

E: No. I asked you to do it later.
    oh no (okay?)
  (E and S talk)
    (D makes noises; ay, etc.)
    uh uh boo
    open!
    (pause)
    uh open!

S: (mimicing) uh-oo!
    uh
    uh open! (these times, she means
     close)

E: Hey.
S: (talking softly to E)
E: (talking)
E: I think this could go on all night.
    open!
    ——————————

    (walking to where keys are)
    Kay.

E: Okay?
S: I think she said case.
    uh oi
E: Don't touch. Don't.
  (phone rings)
    (D follows S out)
E: Deanna (calling)
    Huh
    dah
    uh (etc.)
    uh key
    pay
    uh

  (S hangs up phone)
S: What do you want?
  (E interrupts to ask time)
    no (S taking her hand)
S: Come on.
    no
S: No. no-no.
    nuh
S: Don't come on.
    no (whine)
S: Come on, in.
    no (crying)
    uh no

S: . . . Ain't nobody gonna bother you.
  Not at all.
    (D cries)

JORDAN

1st observation, age 21 months 11 days

(at beginning, will not talk at all, hides head and cries)

    (M showing him pictures in book)
M: There's the ball
    baw

M: And there's the cow. The cow says
   moo.   moo!

M: . . . the cow. Say moo!   moo!
   (E talks to M, J sees picture of
   cat)

M: What does the cat say?   meow
   Meow   uh

M: What does the cat say?   yadoe uh (more babble)

M: This? Cow. That's the train.
   See train. It goes choo choo.   uh
                               uh
                               uh (reaching for t.r.)

M: No, she's not . . . See the house.
   See the house. Nice house.   uh ha! (he pets it)
                               (sees a horse) Naa noo (pets)

M: Nice horse. Nice horse.   ah noo

M: See the pretty flowers. Smell the
   flowers. Smell them. (they both
   do)

E: Do the flowers smell good?

M: Jordan, do you want a bite?   mm
                                 gay

   Give me a bite. (he does)

M: Oh, say hi. Hi. Hi poppy. Say
   hi nana.   ah nana

M: Hi nana! Say hi poppy. Hi.   pop-uh ehe

E: Poppy's got a ball.

M: Poppy's ball. Say ball.   ⎰ mama (soft)
                                ⎱ ball (touches picture)[1]

M: Ball, poppy has a ball. Oh, look
   at that. See the bird.   Bir!
                                 ⎰ ah
                                 ⎱ bir

M: Hi Bird. Where is the bell?   uh mommy

M: See the bell.

                 ——————————————(cont.)——————————————

                               ma
                               ma (grabs cheese from M)

E: He's hungry. Are you starving the
   boy?   muh muh mh muh
                               ma
                               ma
                               uh
                               oh mama

[1] Brackets indicate sequences of holophrases, as defined in the text.

	(pause) then repeats above sequence
	mommy
	ma
M: There!	ma!
	ma
	muh
	uh mommy

$\left\{ \begin{array}{l} \text{uh} \\ \text{duck (reaching for book with} \end{array} \right.$
picture of duck in it) (pause)
$\left\{ \begin{array}{l} \text{dah! (opens it, points)} \\ \text{duh} \\ \text{dah (pause)} \end{array} \right.$
Duh

M: Quack quack	uh
M: Ooh. See the policeman's cat.	
Meow.	mya
M: Meow. That's a little duck. No.	dah! (pointing to duck)
Yes it is.	

book (as M turns pages)
$\left\{ \begin{array}{l} \text{oy (pause)} \\ \text{ush} \\ \text{ma} \\ \text{iish} \\ \text{book (pauses all through here)} \end{array} \right.$

M: . . . kitty.	uh ooo muh
M: No?	nuh
M: Oh, see the bell. Ding dong.	oof
	ah (pause)
	duh!
	uh uh
	uh
	muh

$\left\{ \begin{array}{l} \text{uh} \\ \text{duck} \\ \text{ah!} \end{array} \right.$

| M: Yeah. | $\left\{ \begin{array}{l} \text{duh-uh} \\ \text{duhuh} \\ \text{nuhuh} \end{array} \right.$ |

M: Meow.

FELICE

1st observation, age 17 months 20 days

(O is present. E and O have been here about 15 minutes, playing with Felice, who will not talk to them. M is in the kitchen typing. Joyce (Paula's mother) has come to door, and has coaxed Felice into talking. Joyce is leaving.

	bye-bye
(E and Joyce talk, Joyce leaves)	
	bye Joyce
E: (repeating) Bye Joyce	
M: (talks to E)	
E: Bye Joyce	
M: Can you say good-bye to Joyce? Did you say good-bye to Joyce?	
	Joyce
M: Where did Joyce go, Felice?	
	bye-bye
M: Right.	
E: Where's Paula? Where's Paula, Felice? Right. (mumble)	(she points)
	keys(?) (very softly)
E: Where's what? Keys? All right. Keys.	
	keys
(E and M talk)	
	toy (touching E's purse)
E: Yeah, it's a purse.	

	(pulling things out of E's purse) keys
E: Yeah	
	book (holding E's wallet)
E: It's like a book (etc.).	
	pees pees (picks up E's glass case)
E: Un-uh. Un-uh. No. Here, take this (hands her something else, she reaches for glasses). (E shakes head) I'm sorry. I'm a very cruel lady. No.	
	eyes (still looking at glasses)
Not I, glasses.	
M: I think she said eyes.	
E: Oh. Did you say eyes? (E talks)	
	(still playing in purse, she wants more things) maw maw

E: You're getting yourself all dirty.
   (she is holding candy) No more.   cany
   Mommy won't let us come back.

                                 um (low)
                                 (she pulls out a stick of gum)
                                 keys

M: No, that's gum

                                 gum

M: Yeah.

                                 gum

E: Put it back. (she does)
M: Say thank you
   (E and M interchange) What is that?   keys
                                 mommy!

M: What?

                                 book (she is looking through E's
                                 charge cards)

M: Give it back to the girl.
                       _____

                                 (walking to M, very softly)
                                 hi mom

M: Hi mommy.

                                 cu cu clock! (picked up toy car)
                                 cu cu-

M: What is that?

                                 clock (cock)

M: No.
E: (talking to **M**)

                                 no-oh
   (E and M talk)

                                 coo coo clock (She is 'driving' car
                                 on table)

M: No.
E: It's not a cuckoo clock. It's
   a car.

                                 car
E: Mm-hm.   coo coo clock
   (M and E laugh)
E: Cuckoo clock. She hears it.
   (a clock *is* ticking loudly)

                                 cuckoo
                     _____

                                 (in kitchen, near high chair)
                                 up

E: Oh, you wanta go up there.
   Is that why you said up?
   (E and M talk, F very quiet)

E: We're going to go bye-bye.
M: Say bye, baby.

                                        bye!
(E and M talk)

                                        bye!
(E and M laugh)   bye!
                                        bye!

Appendix B   Sample transcripts: training sessions

GLYNIS

2nd training session, age 17 months 0 days

	(runs into bedroom)
	doll
	doll
	doll
E: Doll?	mm doll
	doll
	doll
E: Who wants a doll?	do-ll
	doll
E: Glynis wants the doll.	uh doll

E: Glynis doll. Come on. Do you wanna see what I've got? Look at the clown. Com'ere. The tape can't hear you from that far.	{ doll
	  mommy
	  mm

E: Oh, mommy won't let anything bad happen to you.	
E: Look. Clown.	uh uh cun (might have been tyring to say clown)
E: Do you wanta do it? Say Glynis clown. Glynis turns the clown on.	uh cownun (E turns it on and off)
E: On. Clown on. Say clown on.	cla
E: Off? Clown off.	on
E: Clown on.	
E: (pause) She doesn't know quite what to make of it. Ever see anything like that before?	{ da da oh da ah
E: What?	doll
E: Doll. Glynis wants the doll.	

Glynis doll. Where's the doll, Glynis?	uh uh doll (she is pointing at doll shelf)
E: Where's the doll?	oh oh doll
E: (to M) You don't want her to have one of those, do you?	
M: One of what?	
E: Those paper dolls. She's in there again.	
M: One of these?	(from other room, soft)
	⎰ do
	⎱ uh ee doll
M: She can have a little . . .	⎧ dah
	⎨ dah
	⎩ dah da da (screamed)
M: Okay, here it is. Here it is. Box.	box (baby?)
M: Come here. Well, I've got the box here.	⎰ hah
	⎱ bah bah bah! (screamed)
M: I've got the box here.	
E: The box is here, Glynis. Box here.	
M: Here they are.	⎰ no!
	⎱ buh!
M: You wanna give me that candy?	
	(cont.)

---

	uh da (playing with ball)
	boom (as she climbs down from chair)
M: (telling about G climbing chair)	
M: (G is rocking in chair) Is that rock-a-bye?	
M: How do you sing rock a bye baby? Will you sing rockabye baby? (E talking same time)	um ah mm (singing)
M: Will you sing rockabye baby now?	mm (very soft)
M: No.	
E: What are you doing, Glynis?	no
E: No? You know, you say that better than anybody else I know.	bum
M: (G is smiling) Was that funny?	(laughs)
M: Hmm? Very funny?	(both laugh)
M: Are you gonna rock yourself right off?	
E: If you do, you'll hit the table.	
M: Now can you sing rockabye?	(still laughing)

M: (notices G's doll) Oh, that looks like
   a little kiddle doll.
E: (reaching for it) What's that?   don't doll.
E: Don't doll? You don't want me to
   touch the doll?   no
E: Say don't touch.

                                                (cont.)

                                                (G is holding a stuffed animal; she
                                                calls them all gaga or gaca)
E: What are you doing, Glynis?   gaga oh gaga
                                                ooh
                                                ey
M: What have you got there?   aygah (sounds like I got)
M: Yeah. Is that nice?   (she hugs it)
    Aw, you love it.   ah
    Aw.   uh (looking at the end of her finger)
    You?
M: Yes, you got your finger back,
   didn't you?   waa!
M: Yes.   ah! (screamed)
M: Yes. It just fits. On. Mm hm.

                                                ah goo (another scream)
M: Did you put it on?   ahhh (sounds like trying to say on.)
M: On.   ah! (scream)
M: Yes.   no
M: (to E) ... are you getting that?

                                                eye!
M: Yes?   eye
E: You're getting to be a real ham,
   Glynis.   uh (scream)
                                                on! (screamed, but clear − she has
                                                   an animal on the tip of her finger)
                                                bon! (screamed)
M: Mm hm.   ⎰ bine
M: Mm hm.   ⎱ ooh whee!
M: Oo whee   da off (hugging it)
M: Aw. Do you love it? Is it nice?   oh da
                                                ooh dee dee dee dee
                                                ah
M: Aw.   ⎧ ay
M: Down.   ⎨ dun
                                                ⎩ book
                                                ⎧ ook
                                                ⎨ ow
                                                ⎩ down!

E: (very loud) Down. The book goes
   down. Book down.   book down

E: Good.

M: She said it. She said it.

E: Oh Glynis. You're terrific! Book
   down.   mama

M: Yes?   ⎰doddy
                            ⎱doddy (another doorbell is ringing)

M: No, that's not daddy. She hears
   the bell ringing out there. No, that's
   not daddy coming. It's early yet.

E: Daddy home? Daddy home.   daddy ohah

M: Yeah. That's not daddy. That's
   somebody else's bell.   daddy

M: Yeah.   daddy mommy

M No, that's not daddy.   uh mommy uh (kind of contorted)

M. No, that's not daddy.   un-uh
                      daddy un

M: It's not even Anne.   ommy da-ay

O: I?   mommy
                      daddy

M: No, that's not daddy.

E: Somebody's at the door, huh?
   Somebody door.

                   (cont.)

               (Glynis is stretching doll's scarf;
                E thinks it's Anne's)

E: Whose scarf is that, Glynis?
   Whose scarf is that?   hee (laughing)
                      baa! (screaming)

E: Is that Anne's scarf?   ow!

M: Ow?   ow doll!

M: Well, who wears it? Who wears the
   scarf? Now don't stretch it so much
   and it won't stretch out of shape.
   Who wears that scarf?   doll
                      doll!

E: That's right. That's the doll's?

E: Is it?

M: Mm hm.

E: Very good.

E: Doll's scarf.   uh! (very loud)
                      uh!

M: Well, go get a doll to put the scarf
   on.

E: (laughing) It'll have to be a very
   big doll by the time she's done with
   it.

M: (laughing) yeah. A doll with a very
   wide skinny, uh wide short neck.

                                     ⎧ mommy ow
                                     ⎨ dowoo
                                     ⎩ stut

E: . . . don't you have a doll? Here's a
   doll. Look.
                                    no (on tape, almost sounds like doll)

E: No? Say no doll. (she is walking
   away) Come on back.
                                     uh doll
                                     mommy

E: Here's mommy.

M: I'm right here.

E: Mommy's on the sofa.
                                    ⎰ doll
                                    ⎱ doll

E: (mimicing) A doll. A doll. A doll.
                                     doll

E: Say I want a doll
                                     niiii! (=nice)

                                     (cont.)

---

                                     beebee

M: Why are you sucking your thumb?

                                    ⎧ ooh bobboo (=bottle)
                                    ⎨ bobbo
                                    ⎪ baa
M: Are you thirsty?
                                    ⎩ bobboo

E: Bottle?

M: (unintelligible) . . . Well, where is it?
   Where did you leave it? Do you
   remember?

E: Where's the bottle?
                                     bottle   baa

E: Where is the bottle?
                                     hm
                                     no-o

E: No bottle.
                                     uh uh uh (etc.) (ends in buh)

M: What do you see there?

M: (unintelligible) (G goes to piano) Are
   you gonna sing for your supper?   huh
                                     bee

   (M and E talk while G plays)

E: Glynis (calling) What are you doing?

                                     (playing with scarf; it falls)
                                     oop down

M: Oop down.

E: Scarf down.
E: Scarf fell down.
   (M to E and back)

uh.
uh
uh (etc.)
boo
uh (she is pulling on the scarf)

M: That poor little scarf has never in all
   these years gotten such a workout.
   (goes on about scarf)
M: Oh. What's that? Is that a drawer?

diiy

M: Yeah. Do you like to open little
   drawers and peer into them?

No

M: Yes you do.

ayy nuh duhla
hi!
hi!

E: Say Hi Maris. Hi Maris.
E: Hi Glynis.
E: Boom?
E: Who goes boom?

(laughs)
bum
buml
ah uh (guttural noises)
ha!
bum! (screamed loud)

(G falls) E: Ooh!

   ⎰ah
   ⎱boom
    down
    uh down (crying)

M: What's the matter?
M: Chair? Is the chair crooked?

  (crying) dun

   (cont.)

E: Bye bye.

bye bye
bah bye
bah bye.

E: Bye bye. Bye bye Maris, say.
   Bye bye Maris.
E: (mimics her)
E: (mimics again)
E: Did they say something to . . .
   (everybody laughs)

mum goo (etc.)
ummnun

nah

E: That'll teach me, huh?

⎰me
⎱bun

E: Bye?
E: Bye bye – Glynis.

Bye bye
⎰dum
⎱dum (with toy telephone)

E: Ding ding. Hello. Ding ding. Say
   hello. Don't you answer the phone

when it rings? Hello. Hello Glynis. Bye bye Glynis.	um hi!
E: (laughing) Ooh! You're gonna break the phone. (pause) Hello, Glynis. (E and M, soft) (long pause)	(E is playing with Glynis) ho!
E: Hello.	oop down (phone dropped) oop down

FELICE

1st training session, age 17 months 24 days

(E trying to get F to sing)	happy birthday (singing)
E: Oh, there she goes. Go on. All right. Mommy'll sing too.	
M: To daddy. Happy Birthday to – Happy Birthday to – daddy. Happy Birthday to – Well? Happy Birthday to daddy, Felice?	da-y?
M: Huh?	
E: Yeah. (laughing) You know that you're terrific. Don't look at me with that smile. I think you're terrific.	(she laughs)
E: Go bring me your teddy bear, Felice.	

	(F brings in toy radio)
E: Oh! Felice's radio.	rayo (?)
E: Radio.	
E: (listening) Does the radio make music?	music
E: Radio makes music . . .	ooh
E: Make nice. Nice, Felice. Nice. Can you dance? Can Felice dance? Let's see Felice dance . . . dance. What's in there?	
E: Maris's purse. Maris purse . . . She says pees, purse. What's that?	pees (holding E's purse) key (she is holding it)
E: Key.	dahor
E: Door. Keys open the door. Go open door. Open door. (she does) Thank you. (she gets O's purse) I think we'd better stick to one purse. You can have everything in . . . That one's for Carrie. Here, come play with this one.	pees
E: What is it?	pees

E: Purse. Maris purse. You can say my name. Show Carrie how you can say Maris. Say Maris.	Mare.
	(cont.)
	(looking at pictures) daddy
E: Is that daddy? Does that look like daddy?	daddy
	omma
	daddy
	uh
	(F keeps making uh uh noises)
(too soft)	
	(picked up comb) bush
E: Brush. That's Carrie's brush	uh uh
O: Brush hair.	hair
O: . . . hair	hair
	hair
	here (hands E comb)
E: Thank you . . . Say hair. Hair. (F is combing hair)	
E: Oh pretty.	pretty
(very soft to O) Let's do that, Okay? Peek-a-boo . . . Peek-a-boo. Peek-a-boo.	huh
E: Peek-a-boo.	
	(trying to open pen) uh open
	opoo opoo
	opoo opoo
E: Open pen.	pen (very soft)
E: Open pen.	pen
E: Open pen.	opu peuh
E: Opu pen! Now. Please give . . . paper . . . Don't you get that on there. (she is trying to write all over things)	
	ahpuh
	oh pen (E is talking softly)
E: That's the keys. Look. Open keys.	opoo opoo
	⎧ opoo
	⎨ (keys) (?)
E: Say open keys.	⎩ opoo kes

E: Open *keys*.   opoo keys
E: Good girl!   hmm
                                               umuh

---

                                               uh opoo (handing to M)
M: No, that's Carrie's.   ⎰ uh uh
                                               ⎱ Carrie oooo
                                               ees (=Felice)
                                               ees
                                               ees (wants to see picture she thinks
                                                  is her)
E: Oh, you wanta see Ees? Say, look
   at Ees.   ⎧ ees
                                               ⎨ ees
                                               ⎩ look ah ah
                                               ah
                                               ees ees
                                               uh uh
E: (to O) You just made her so   (with a tube of lipstick
   happy . . .   opu opu opu
E: That's 'open lipstick'.   ipstick
E: Open lipstick.   ee lips
E: Yech. Forget it (she sticks her hand
   in the lipstick) . . .   book
O: What? Put the cover back on? Okay
E: Look.   bah
E: Look Felice . . . Hey Felice. You
   don't want it? Say open purse.   opu ur
E: What do you open? What do you
   open?   opu
M: Wai-wai-wait!   (to Carrie)
                                               Carrie
O: No . . .
                                               opu opu (holding tape box)
O: Open box.
E: Good girl   ee
                                               shoe (holding E's shoe)
E: (to M, who is cleaning) Tired?
M: I'm not through yet.   shoe
E: Shoe. Maris's shoe. Say Maris.   mah
   Maris shoe.   (unintelligible)
E: Maris shoe. Good. Put my shoe on
   my foot.   boo (as she does it)
E: Thank you.
E: See?   (laugh)
                                               ee

Mar uh uh (taking shoe off)

E: Oh. Are you gonna put my shoes on
    and take em off? This is a very silly
    game. All gone. (M soft)   uh
                                            oof

    (M and E talk)
E: . . . my shoes. Leave em alone. Leave
    em alone.   mah
                                   { opu
                                   { urse

E: Oh good girl! She said open purse.
    (E to O)
E: (F is looking at flowers) Flowers
                              fala (= flower)
                              uh

    (O asks E a question)

Combinatorial speech and
sequences of holophrases for all
ten subjects – representative
examples

COMBINATIONS   SEQUENCES

Lia

Observation

$\left\{\begin{array}{l}\text{daggie } (=\text{doggie}) \\ \text{daggie} \\ \text{woof woof} \\ \text{woof woof}\end{array}\right.$

$\left\{\begin{array}{l}\text{dah } (=\text{train}) \\ \text{dah} \\ \text{awgaw } (=\text{all gone})\end{array}\right.$

$\left\{\begin{array}{l}\text{book} \\ \text{baby} \\ \text{book}\end{array}\right.$

$\left\{\begin{array}{l}\text{juice (water for iron)} \\ \text{hot} \\ \text{mm ga} \\ \text{ga}\end{array}\right.$

Training
guhiy (=go outside) bye-bye
bye-bye cow (=clown)
see cow
go bye-bye
bye da (=train) (said as train went
  by)
bye buk (=truck) (said as truck went
  by)
bai (=pants) daddy
bai (=pants) mommy
my mommy

$\left\{\begin{array}{l}\text{mooo!} \\ \text{cah } (=\text{cow})\end{array}\right.$

$\left\{\begin{array}{l}\text{ah moo} \\ \text{ca-ah } (=\text{cow})\end{array}\right.$

$\left\{\begin{array}{l}\text{awgaw} \\ \text{bip } (=\text{beep}) \text{ (she is beeping clown's} \\ \quad \text{nose)}\end{array}\right.$

$\left\{\begin{array}{l}\text{duh } (=\text{train}) \\ \text{awgaw}\end{array}\right.$

$\left\{\begin{array}{l}\text{a girl} \\ \text{book}\end{array}\right.$

$\left\{\begin{array}{l}\text{bye} \\ \text{light} \\ \text{ight} \\ \text{light}\end{array}\right.$

COMBINATIONS

SEQUENCES

{ ight (=light)
  allaw (=all gone)

{ bai (=pants or clothes)
  daddy

{ bish (=fish)
  baa (=bath)

{ bai (=clothes)
  bai
  dagee (=daddy)

Deanna

Observation

{ open
  purse

{ purse
  open

{ huh
  open
  purse
  purse
  open
  open

Training
open box

{ dop (=stop)
  cown (clown)

{ mommy
  eye

{ cown
  dop

{ matches
  open
  icky

{ bye
  Buck (a man's name)

{ box
  open

{ doggie
  bye bye

{ button
  berty (=pretty)

{ buh (=bus)
  guh
  gone gone

COMBINATIONS   SEQUENCES

Glynis

Observation

go baby   ⎰ duh (=down)
oo buh buh bye mom   ⎱ me
bye bye baby cuh   ⎰ baby
bye ma   ⎱ go bee
no mama   ⎧ baby
daddy doll   ⎨ hi
                                          ⎩ baby
                                          ⎰ bye
                                          ⎱ baby
                                          ⎰ nuh (=no)
                                          ⎱ dah-dee (=thank you)
                                          ⎧ ball
                                          ⎨ da (=doll)
                                          ⎩ ball
                                          ⎧ doll
                                          ⎨ ball
                                          ⎩ dow (=down)

Training

don't doll   ⎧ ook (=book)
book down   ⎨ ow
bye-bye ma   ⎩ down
beebee (=baby) gaga (=animal)   ⎰ nah
bee bee bee gaga   ⎱ daddy
baby gaga   ⎰ daddy
dah-di (=daddy) home   ⎱ no
ma ball   ⎧ muh (=my)
my doll   ⎨ doll
uh my doll   ⎩ duh (=down)
                                          ⎧ dah
                                          ⎨ di
                                          ⎩ hoo (=daddy home)
                                          ⎧ cookie
                                          ⎨ go
                                          ⎩ allgone

Katie

Observation

o   o

Training

oorollball (=roll ball, run together)   ⎧ pah
oorodaball (=roll ball, run together)   ⎨ pah
pay pah (=play purse)   ⎩ pah pah pur (=play purse)

COMBINATIONS   SEQUENCES

pay pah pur (=play purse)   { pah (=purse)
baa ow (=baby eye)   { pay ah (=play)
du ahyah (=doggie eye)

Jordan

Observation
ah (=hi) nana
oh-pen key
noo (=no) mama

Training
up duck   { light
Juh dah (=Jordan down)   { on
ah lights on (=are)   { uh
daddy olive   { li (=light)
                                     { off
                                     { mommy
                                     { home
                                     { mommy
                                     { bye-bye

Jessica

Observation
go get it   { mommy
be careful   { book
pen ca (=pen color)   { doey (=dolly)
pen ca   { wet
pee ca
uh uh pen ca
oopuh bok (=open box)
buk eeup (=book up)
mom cap (=mommy cup)
baygoo ah (=bathing suit on)
who wet
good girl

Training
ca no (=clown nose)   { gookie (=cookie)
go woof   { awgo (=all gone)
doggie woof   { gookie
bah Kukky (=bye Kathy)   { uh buh (=boy)
bah Kukky   { bye buh
ah da-y come (=daddy come)   { uh buh buh
milk cucup (=cup)   { milk
su ah ah foot (=socks on foot)   { cup

COMBINATIONS	SEQUENCES

so ah (=socks on)
read book
read book

Andrew

Observation

thisis nice	{ boat
big car	{ where
beeguh (=big) uh boat	

Training

| potty down | { chair |
| my shoe | { duck (=stuck) |

Ricky

Observation

my mommy	{ bluh (=blow)
you mommy	{ no (= nose)
ee uh mom	⎰ uh milk
ohoo more cup	{ me
beep beep car	⎱ mommy
bye bye ma	{ uh milkuh
no uhmommy	{ mama
	{ mom
	{ milkuh
	{ mom
	{ milk
	⎰ uh beep beep
	{ mom
	⎱ beep beep car

Training

daddy come wahuh agah	⎰ cock (=clock)
me doll	{ cock
no money	⎱ no
money go	⎰ bum (=boom)
no more money	{ bum
mm mommy's pilluh (=pillow)	⎱ bok (=book) bum
bok bum (=book boom)	⎰ muhbok (=mailbox)
bye bye mommy	{ ok
bye bye daddy	{ uhmuk
bye bye daddy	⎱ no
bye bye mommy	{ ee book
bye bye Maruh (=Maris)	{ mommy

COMBINATIONS

SEQUENCES

disisduh purse (=this is the purse)
disuh buruh (=this a brush)
diss is uh (=this is a)
bye bye pur (=purse)
uh no milk

{ mommy
no
mommy

{ no
ubby (=Bubby)
bay
bye

Paula

Observation
book uh mommy
oi doiuh awee (=oi door Larry)

{ mmom
mama
puppa (=poppa)

{ mommy
mom
oh

{ pretty
douh (=coat)
douh
uh uh uh

Training
dolly uhdawk (=talks)
doggie talks
doggie duck
doggie talks
doggie duck

{ chicken
soup

{ clown
uh bub (=pop)
uh bub

{ doggie
doggie
head

Felice

Observation
bye Joyce
hi mom
Happy birthday daddy
Happy birthday Arry (=Harry)
Happy birthday Arry
Happy birthday Arry
Happy birthday Arry
Happy birthday
Happy birthday daddy
Happy birthday Arry

{ up
ubbie (=Bubby)
horsie

COMBINATIONS   SEQUENCES

Happy birthday
Happy birthday daddy
Happy birthday daddy
Happy birthday
Happy birthday

Training
open pen   ⎧ daddy
opu peuh (=open pen)   ⎪ omma
opoo kes (open keys)   ⎨ daddy
opoo keys   ⎩ uh
opu ur (=open purse)   ⎧ opoo
opu ox (=open box)   ⎩ keys
opoo pen   ⎧ ees (=Felice)
opoo peuh (=pen)   ⎨ ees
Happy birthday   ⎩ look ah ah
Happy birthday Wary (=Larry)   ⎧ Mah
opoo os (=open box)   ⎨ opoo
oh op opee ur (=open purse)   ⎩ urse
o-poo boom (=pen)   ⎧ opoo opoo
opoo pees (=purse)   ⎪ bock
opoo ur (=purse)   ⎨ bock
o (=open) box   ⎩ bock (=box)
hi Bubby   ⎧ oh
hi Bubby   ⎪ hereuh (=here)
Happy birthday Arry   ⎨ ay
open bok (=box)   ⎩ dolly
opoo pees
here mommy
book daddy
daddy book
opoo box
here daddy
cookies box
cookies box
read book
read book

Appendix D Sample coding sheets: Jordan. Observations 1 and 2

(1)

Subject __Jordan__   Age _____   Session _____

b.d. _____   Coded by _____   Date _____

Subject-verb-object	Holophrastic usage					Non-holophrastic usage		
	Locative	Possessive	I want	Negative	Other	Naming	Repetition	Other
Obs. #1								
							(=ball) baw	
							mo	
							moo	
						meow		
							(=house) uh ha	
							popuh-ehe	
								mama
							ball	
							(=bird) bir	
								uh mommy
								ma
								ma
								ma
								ma
								uh mama
								mommy
								ma
								ma
								muh
								uh mommy
			uh duck					

Note:

(2)

Subject __Jordan__   Age _____   Session _____

b.d. _____   Coded by _____   Date _____

| Subject-verb-object | Holophrastic usage | | | | | Non-holophrastic usage | | |
	Locative	Possessive	I want	Negative	Other	Naming	Repetition	Other
						(=duck) dah		
						duh		
						dah		
						duh		
						dah		
						(=fish) bish		
								ma
						book		
						(=duck) duh		
							muh	
						duck		
						duckuh		
						duckuh		
Obs. #2								
						(=ball) uh bah		
							iy mom	
							ma	
uh baw								
uh ball								
						bah		
(=ball) uh buh buh								
(=ball) bah								

Note:

(3)

Subject __Jordan__   Age _____   Session _____

b.d. _____   Coded by _____   Date _____

Subject-verb-object	Holophrastic usage					Non-holophrastic usage		
	Locative	Possessive	I want	Negative	Other	Naming	Repetition	Other
			ah ah bah					
			(=ball) baw					
			bah					
			bah					
			ball					
			ball					
			ball					
							(=ball) booo	
							bah	
							uh ball	
							bahoo	
			upah					
					up			
					up			
						duck		
						duck		
						ayah duck		
							moo	
							moo	
							moo	

Note:

(4)

Subject __Jordan__   Age _____   Session _____

b.d. _____   Coded by _____   Date _____

| | Holophrastic usage | | | | | Non-holophrastic usage | | |
Subject-verb-object	Locative	Possessive	I want	Negative	Other	Naming	Repetition	Other
							mih	
							muh	
							muh	
(⁻pen) pe								
						(=pen) pe		
						pe		
						paperuh		
							(=pussy cat) pucot	
doit								
						(=purr= pussy cat) uhperper		
						per		
(=ball) ma baw								
						(=Sonny) onny		
						onny		
shut up								
					boom			
					boom			
								uh dock
							(=box) buh	
								mama
								ma
						ow pen		

Note:

References

Antinucci, Francesco and Parisi, Domenico. (1973). Early language acquisition: a model and some data. In C. Ferguson and D. Slobin (eds.), *Studies of child language development*. New York: Holt, Rinehart, and Winston.

Austin, J. L. (1965). *How to do things with words*. New York: Oxford University Press.

Bellugi, Ursula and Brown, Roger (eds.). (1964). The acquisition of language. *Monographs of the Society for Research in Child Development*, **29** (1).

Bijou, S. and Baer, D. (1965). *Child development II: universal stage of infancy*. New York: Appleton, Century, Crofts.

Bloom, Lois. (1970). *Language development: form and function in emerging grammars*. Research monograph, **59**. Cambridge, Mass.: MIT Press.

Bloom, Lois. (1973). *One word at a time*. The Hague: Mouton.

Bloom, Lois, Hood, Lois, and Lightbown, Patsy. (1974). Imitation in language development: if, when, and why. *Cognitive Psychology*, **6**, 380–420.

Braine, M. D. S. (1963). The ontogeny of English phrase structure: the first phase. *Language*, **39**, 1–13.

Brown, Roger. (1958). *Words and things*. Glencoe, Illinois: Free Press.

Brown, Roger. (1973). *A first language*. Cambridge, Mass.: Harvard University Press.

Brown, Roger, Bellugi, Ursula, and Cazden, Courtney. (1968). The child's grammar from I to III. In J. P. Hill (ed.), *The 1967 Minnesota Symposium on Child Psychology*, pp. 28–73. Minneapolis: University of Minnesota Press.

Bruner, Jerome S., Olver, Rose R., and Greenfield, Patricia. (1966). *Studies in cognitive growth*. New York: Wiley and Sons.

Chomsky, Noam. (1957). *Syntactic structures*. The Hague: Mouton Press.

Chomsky, Noam. (1965). *Aspects of the theory of syntax*. Cambridge, Mass.: MIT Press.

Chomsky, Noam. (1968). *Language and mind*. New York: Harcourt, Brace & World.

De Laguna, Grace. (1927). *Speech: Its functions and development*. New Haven, Conn.: Yale University Press.

Dore, John. (1973). *The development of speech acts*. Unpublished doctoral dissertation, Rockefeller University.

Ervin, Susan. (1964). Imitation and structural change in children's language. In E. H. Lenneberg (ed.), *New directions in the study of language*. Cambridge, Mass.: MIT Press.

Fillmore, Charles. (1968). The case for case. In Emmon W. Bach and Robert T. Harms (eds.), *Universals of linguistic theory*. New York: Holt, Rinehart, and Winston.

Greenfield, Patricia. (1967). *Who is 'dada'?* Unpublished paper, Syracuse University.

Greenfield, Patricia. (1968). *Development of the holophrase: observation on Lauren Greenfield*. Unpublished paper, Harvard University, Center for cognitive studies.

Greenfield, Patricia Marks, Nelson, Karen, and Saltzman, Elliot. (1972). The development of rulebound strategies for manipulating seriated cups: a parallel between action and grammar. *Cognitive Psychology*, **3**, 291–310.

Greenfield, Patricia Marks, Smith, Joshua H., and Laufer, Bernice. (In press). *Communication and the beginning of language: the development of semantic structure in one-word speech and beyond*. New York: Academic Press.

Gregoire, A. (1937). *L'apprentissage du language: les deux premières annés*, 1. Paris: Droz.

Gruber, Jeffrey S. (1967). Topicalization in child language. *Foundations of Language*, **3** (1), 37–65.

Kaye, Kenneth P. (1968). *Developmental origins of predication*. Unpublished paper, Harvard University.

Lashley, K. S. (1951). The problem of serial order in behavior. In L. A. Jeffress (ed.), *Cerebral mechanisms in behavior*, pp. 112–36. New York: Wiley.

Leopold, W. F. (1949). *Speech development of a bilingual child*, III. Illinois: Northwestern University Press.

MacNamara, John. (1972). Cognitive basis of language learning in infants. *Psychological Review*, **79** (1), 1–13.

McCarthy, Dorothea. (1954). Language development in children. In L. Carmichael (ed.), *Manual of child psychology*, pp. 492–630. New York: Wiley.

McCawley, James. (1968). The role of semantics in grammar. In E. Bach and R. Harms (eds.), *Universals in linguistic theory*, pp. 124–69. New York: Holt, Rinehart, and Winston.

McNeill, David. (1966). Developmental psycholinguistics. In F. Smith and G. Miller (eds.), *The genesis of language*, pp. 1–91. Cambridge, Mass.: MIT Press.

McNeill, David. (1968). On theories of language acquisition. In T. Dixon and D. Horton (eds.), *Verbal behavior and general behavior theory*, pp. 406–20. Englewood Cliffs, N.J.: Prentice-Hall.

McNeill, David. (1970a). The development of language. In Paul H. Mussen (ed.), *Carmichael's manual of child psychology*, I, New York: Wiley.

McNeill, David. (1970b). *The acquisition of language: The study of developmental psycholinguistics*. New York: Harper and Row.

McNeill, David. (1972). Personal communication.

McNeill, David. (1971). *Two fold way for speech*. Paper presented to CNRS Conference on Psycholinguistics, December 1971.

McNeill, David. (1974). Semiotic extension. Paper presented to Loyola Symposium on cognition, April 1974.

Miller, George and Ervin, Susan. (1964). The development of grammar in child language. In U. Bellugi and R. Brown (eds.), *The acquisition of language.* SRCD Monograph **29** (1), 9–34. Chicago: University of Chicago Press.

Mowrer, O. H. (1960). *Learning theory and the symbolic processes.* New York: Wiley.

Nelson, Katherine. (1973). Structure and strategy in learning to talk. *Monographs of the Society for Research in Child Development,* **38** (1–2) (serial no. 149).

Nelson, Katherine. (1974). Concepts, word, and sentence: interrelations in acquisition and development. *Psychological Review,* **81** (4), 267–85.

Piaget, Jean. (1952). *The origins of intelligence in children.* New York: Norton Library.

Piaget, Jean. (1962). *Play, dreams, and imitation in childhood.* New York: Norton Library.

Rodgon, Maris and Kurdek, Lawrence. (1975). Vocal and gestural imitation in children two years and under. Paper presented to the American Psychological Association, Chicago.

Ryan, Joanna. (1973). Interpretation and imitation in early language development. In R. A. Hinde and T. Hinde-Stevenson (eds.), *Constraints on learning: limitations and predispositions,* pp. 427–43. London: Academic Press.

Schlesinger, I. M. (1971). Production of utterances and language acquisition. In D. I. Slobin (ed.), *The ontogenesis of grammar,* pp. 63–101. New York: Academic Press.

Shipley, Elizabeth F., Smith, Carlota S., and Gleitman, Lila R. (1969). A study in language acquisition. *Language,* **35**, 322–44.

Sinclair, Hermina. (1971). Sensorimotor action patterns as a condition for the acquisition of syntax. In R. Huxley and E. Imgram (eds.), *Language acquisition: models and methods,* pp. 121–30. New York: Academic Press.

Sinclair-de-Zwart, Hermina. (1969). Developmental psycholinguistics. In D. Elkind and J. Flavell (eds.), *Studies in cognitive development,* pp. 315–36. New York: Oxford University Press.

Sinclair-de-Zwart, Hermina. (No date). Sensory-motor action schemes as a condition of the acquisition of syntax. Unpublished paper.

Sinclair-de-Zwart, Hermina. (1970). The transition from sensory-motor behaviour to symbolic activity. Unpublished paper.

Smith, Joshua H. (1970). The development and structure of holophrases. Unpublished paper, Harvard University, Department of Linguistics.

Stern, Clara and Stern, W. (1907). *Die kindersprache.* Leipzig: Barth.

Vygotsky, Lev S. (1962). *Thought and language.* Cambridge, Mass.: MIT Press.

Werner, Heinz and Kaplan, Bernard. (1963). *Symbol formation.* New York: Wiley.

Index